CW00428495

Study Success

How students get top results in school

---

*The 17 principles that will give you or
your child the drive and tools to succeed!*

Simon Angelo

To all learners, parents and teachers everywhere.
In your hands is our future…

ACCELERATED LEARNING INSTITUTE
Website: www.acceleratedlearn.com
Email: acceleratedlearn@xtra.co.nz
Telephone: +64 9 625 5590

First published by the Accelerated Learning Institute, 2004

10 9 8 7 6 5 4 3 2 1

Copyright © Simon Angelo

All rights reserved. Without limiting the rights under copyright reserved above and except for the purposes of fair reviewing, no part of this publication may be reproduced, stored in or introduced into a retrieval system, or transmitted in any form or by any means (electronic, mechanical, photocopying, recording or otherwise), without the prior written permission of the publisher.

Cover design by Gibson Rusden (www.gibsonrusden.com)

DISCLAIMER
All views, information and estimates in this publication are drawn from many sources, and cannot be verified as accurate. Content is opinion only. Any actions based on this information are entirely the responsibility of the user.

Author Information

A life in empowering people with language training and business communications: Simon Angelo has also taught in Japan and gained recognition for his founding of a technology expo, the development of a consulting web site and the publication of the acclaimed business book "Click & Grow Rich".

Simon gained degrees from The University of Auckland in Commerce (Accounting & Finance), Arts (English Literature) and a Diploma in teaching Speech & Drama from Trinity College London. Upon graduation he established New Zealand's first New Products, Ideas and Innovations Expo, an international event where he helped to showcase some of the country's most exciting new technologies and appeared on numerous television programmes.

Simon went on to set up the Auckland Speech & Drama School where he specialized in teaching Speech & Drama and Effective Communication. Through his work with the Auckland Speech & Drama School, he also pioneered one of the first programmes in New Zealand successfully able to assist people in overcoming ingrained speech and accent habits. For over ten years he successfully entered students in Trinity College London exams, performing arts competitions and castings for film work. In 1997 he traveled extensively throughout Japan both teaching and learning language and culture.

Interested in the rapid growth of the Internet as a teaching and consulting tool, Simon went on to develop an online consulting company with clients worldwide. This led to the publication of his acclaimed business book *Click & Grow Rich* which sold in English and in Korean. He has appeared on a number of television programmes and delivered training seminars based on his book. Simon has also authored a work of fiction, *Tokyo Curry*.

Simon Angelo is available for training, consulting and speaking engagements by appointment. He can be contacted through:

ACCELERATED LEARNING INSTITUTE
Website: www.acceleratedlearn.com
Email: acceleratedlearn@xtra.co.nz
Telephone: +64 9 625 5590

Acknowledgments

Special thanks to my dearest Janet, who with love and support helped me through this project. To my sister Michelle, who inspired me with her dedication as a teacher. To my parents who encouraged me in my own study success. To all my students who provided the inspiration and focus to complete this programme.

Table of Contents

Part III: Accelerated learning and improved memory

Part IV: Specific tools for success

Introduction

Jason isn't his real name but he's a student I've known like so many other students. It's a sunny day and from Jason's bedroom he is lucky enough to have a view of the sea. He is unlucky enough for that view to be a complete distraction. And when he looks out across his desk, it's not the sea that he sees. It's his plans for his car, his relationship with his girlfriend Rebecca and the nagging worry of the English exam tomorrow – in that order.

Jason hates studying for English. Unlike Science or Mathematics, which he's good at, the subject of English could be a foreign language, even though he's spoken it all his life. *Macbeth* began as a pretty cool play with the gruesome murder of a King but as time went by and his English teacher Mr. Clarke started talking about themes and close analysis, Jason lost the plot. The play is open in front of him.

As the sun disappears behind a cloud, Jason's mind wanders. He calculates how many more weekends he will have to work painting for his uncle to buy that new stereo for the car. About six. And there's six of something else soon. Yes, he's been going out with Rebecca for almost six months now! Should he do something for his six-month anniversary? Are you supposed to?

He's dreading the English exam tomorrow. He'll need a good total aggregate score to get into Engineering. If he doesn't what else can he do? And his aggregate would be okay, except for English. Lucky tomorrow is only the practice exam! If only he had the motivation to study. If only he could concentrate his mind and understand what he needed to know before it wandered somewhere else. Anyway, he's been sitting there for fifty minutes now. He's earned a study break. Jason goes downstairs to grab a Coke from the refrigerator and sits in front of the television.

The lounge is empty. His mother is away visiting his grandmother. His sister already moved into her own apartment last year. She's a big shot lawyer now. Went through school with straight A's. Not like him! Half of school for him was like teaching a fish to ride a bicycle.

Chris, Jason's father emerges from the study. He's been studying too. Stuck for ten years at the same level in his job, an MBA through distance learning seemed to be the right step to advancement.

"You get much study done?" Chris asks Jason as he sits on the opposite couch.

"Yeah, quite a lot," Jason lies. "What about you?"

"Quite a lot," Chris lies. But then he admits:

"I tell you something Jason, it's not easy this study, especially when you're trying to learn to analyze financial statements. Me and them just don't get on."

"Yeah, tell me about it. I feel the same way about Shakespeare. It makes no sense these days. I don't know why we still have to study something so out of date."

"If only there was some kind of book. You know, some kind of guide that would tell you how to study and how to do well at it, even when you hated the subject you had to study, like financial statement analysis!"

"You're full of bright ideas aren't you?"

Chris ignores his son's sarcasm. He's old enough to experience parental immunity.

"Do you feel like ordering a pizza for dinner?"

Jason brightens up.

"Yeah, that'd be pretty good."

This programme is a lot like a pizza. It's tasty, delivered to your door and comes in bite size slices. There are seventeen of them. Seventeen principles I've found will contribute to your study success. Yet unlike a pizza instead of adding to your thighs it will add to your mind. Coming up is your first slice – principle one: Stretch your mind.

First, why did I write *Study Success*? I've been teaching people for many years from the ages of 6 to 65 in English, Speech & Drama, Internet technology and Business subjects. Throughout this time I began an exploration into why some students reached the "top of their game" and yet other students just managed to pass, or even fail. I noticed that only about 5 percent of all students seemed to be operating at that top level of achievement. And I wasn't prepared to accept that was all due to IQ - but more about that later. For now, be prepared for this programme to make a difference to the way you think and learn. If you put it into practice and work hard, you could be tomorrow's top student.

If you're anything like the students I've taught over the years, revision books don't excite you. You'd rather be reading Harry Potter, Christopher Pike or the latest Stephen King. So this book is going to be different. It's a ride more than anything. That's right, a cruise through learning and a journey into study success. Beware, this is not a journey for the faint hearted. If you're not up for some real practical mind stretching thinking and you're not prepared to put into action what we're teaching you, give this programme to someone else, because they might one day be your boss...

The best way to benefit from *Study Success* is to read each principle and complete any exercises at the end of the principle immediately after you finish reading. It is recommended that you keep a separate journal for completing the exercises. And it doesn't matter whether you're twelve or one hundred and twelve. The research, findings and exercises here apply to all learners. Mostly this work stems from my own research into why students get top results in school. It comes from my own experience as a student and a teacher. It's also one of the first learning books to apply motivational teachings and principles from the business world to the academic world.

In 2001 when I wrote *Click & Grow Rich*, a business guidebook that went on to enjoy positive reviews, I followed a similarly successful formulae. I had already worked with the internet to produce some revenue streams. Then I sought out those who had been successful and studied them. *Study Success* was a project that stemmed from the belief that in any pursuit, business or otherwise, the most important key success factor is being able to learn well, and being able to learn throughout your entire life.

More than anything else you should take from this guide improved study and learning techniques that will lift your performance in school, be that in the early days of year eight intermediate, to your first year at university, through to later years completing a qualification by distance learning or developing new skills for the corporate world. Life is a changing and evolving process. We often hear anything is possible in life if we put our minds to it. That is true if we have the power and time to learn it first.

Part I: The drive to succeed

Principle 1: Stretch your mind

Perspiration v Inspiration: The 99:1 rule.

Welcome to *Study Success*! We're going to be looking at why around 5 percent of students get the very top results in school, and why the other 95 percent end up doing somewhere between lousy and okay. You may say that some people are just born with more intelligence than others and there's not much more to it: You're a top student when you're three years old or you're not.

But this isn't true! In a moment I'm going to share with you some stories that show why. Yes, there are differences in how quickly some people learn over others, and some people are good at writing while others are better at mathematics. Yet, consider the famous words of Albert Einstein: "Genius is 99 percent perspiration and 1 percent inspiration." Just like at the gym, it's more about how much you sweat with what you've got, than what you've actually got.

Let's take a look at one of the ways we measure IQ for a second. IQ is a universal measure of intelligence and predictor of school performance. One way of measuring IQ is to take your mental age and divide that by your actual age, times one hundred:

$$IQ = \frac{Mental\ Age}{Actual\ Age} \times \frac{100}{1}$$

Say, for instance you are ten years old but you're thinking at the level of an eighteen year old. Since your mental age is eighteen but your actual age is only ten, your IQ would be one hundred and eighty using the above formula. Now there aren't too many ten year olds operating at the level of eighteen year olds, which is why ten year olds don't get to vote or drive cars. Yet consider IQ for a moment. It's something that's constantly changing. If you're ten and you're thinking like an eighteen year old, but five years later you're fifteen and you're still thinking like an eighteen year old, your IQ has actually dropped. That's how the mathematics of the IQ formula work.

At the start, just like in a running race, the way you begin is most important. That's why I want to make a very important point right now:

You can become smarter if you exercise your mind…

Yes, your mind is a muscle. It can become a flabby couch potato best used for opening bags of crisps or a finely tuned machine for precision learning. That's your choice. Maybe you've heard the line I've read often in accelerated learning books: "We only use a tiny fraction of the real potential of our minds". Well that's rather like saying, "Money grows on trees," but not giving any information on where such trees grow or in what season they produce their bounty.

It is difficult tapping these unused landscapes of the mind. However, we can expand our minds by stretching what's already there. A big mind is like a big sweater when it comes to study, it fits all sizes and subjects. And that is principle 1:

The top students succeed in school, not entirely because they're the most intelligent students but because they stretch their minds the most.

Stretching the mind goes back to Einstein's comment on genius being 99 percent perspiration. It takes perspiration to stretch your mind. Reaching a certain level of study success takes some hard work. It is fun and a great challenge.

The Stretching Story

Our story begins on a warm overcast day. For only the second time I was wearing my new high school uniform. The first time had been to try it on. The wool in my blazer smelt fresh. The day was humid as I climbed aboard the bus. This was to be my first day at the Boys' High School. Let me tell you there were lots of nervous new guys on the bus that day. Not the senior students though. They sat looking out the window as if they'd seen it all before. For us "newbies" imagining bullies and homework juggernauts, that bus could have been going to a concentration camp in Nazi Germany. Some of those guys looked like they were on death row. Well, it wasn't that bad but everyone was trying to act tough.

The bus squealed to a halt and the doors opened with a mechanical hiss. Reaching the gate we were immediately ushered into a gigantic assembly hall and made to sit in rows so we could be split into our classes, much like cattle at an auction. This school had a class system in both senses of the term. I forget exactly how the class system worked, but they were ranked from advanced to slow. You could imagine we had classes from A down to K. K for clever. These classes were ranked according to our performance in a test we sat at our old schools.

"Don't worry about which class you begin from," announced the Dean.

But boy were we worried.

He began reading out the names for all the boys who had made the A class. He read up to ten names. Then twenty.

"Where was my name?"

He read up to twenty-eight names. Like so many other boys I was ambitious to be placed in a reasonable class. The A class would have been nice. But where was my name? He read two more names. That was it. Then B. Oh well, being in B, the second best class wouldn't be so bad.

Thirty names were read for B. I wasn't one of them. By this stage I thought I was really heading for the K for clever class. I had flunked that entrance test. The dean announced the boys for C. I wasn't one of them. Finally I was placed in D.

This seems a cruel and harsh system where people are ranked and graded. And it was. Those guys in A were expected to succeed in school, gain advanced qualifications and hold high paying professional positions in later life. Down in K you were expected to know how to dig a hole or mend a fence. It just wasn't right. Yet to this day I am thankful that I wasn't in that top class. Not at first anyway.

For a while I felt very average. I wasn't one of the top performers and maybe I never would be. It put me off trying in school. But then I thought, "no, I'm going to fight this, I'm going to prove myself, and I'm going to turn things around."

I started reading a lot of books about stretching my mind. This was a pretty interesting experiment when you're a thirteen-year-old guy. I read stuff about how to learn and how to increase your IQ. This proved what *Study Success* is all about and what it aims to teach you. When I really began using my mind and flexing its muscles, when I began taking my brain on mental triathlons, it suddenly became more powerful. It wasn't long before teachers started commenting at parent interviews that I'd been put in the wrong class. I wasn't in the wrong class, I'd just learned to stretch my mind. This is principle 1. You can do it too. Soon enough at exam time I'd scored so well that I had climbed up to the equivalent of the A class.

Looking back with the hindsight from what I know now, I can understand what had happened. Basically I'd learned more about how to study and how to learn. I went from an ordinary student to a top student sometimes scoring in the top 5 percent.

They don't rank students so much these days in school. That seems kinder but at the same time determination needs to be encouraged. What I did learn is that even though I was told I was an average student and that everyone else was told to expect average things from me, I said "no, I'm going to do the best I can at this game," and that's what happened.

I hope this has given you some insight into principle 1 – the top students succeed in school because they stretch their minds. They put into action a little bit of mental perspiration. So powerful is this principle that it has been proven in the study of Alzheimer's, that deadly disease where people lose their memory. Studies have found that for every year of education people reduce the risk of Alzheimer's symptoms by 20 percent.

I don't know if you've ever been to a gym but what personal trainers are always telling people about building muscle, is that if you don't use it, you will lose it. The trouble is nobody tells you that about your mind, the strongest, most powerful and flexible muscle that you have in your body. Don't let anyone tell you that your mind is average, because it is not.

> It's not enough to have a good mind. The main thing is to use it well.
> *- Rene Descartes*

You have a great mind but are you using it well? In *Study Success* we're going to teach you how to use it well. And it's not just me teaching you. I want you to exercise the most powerful form of learning known, you teaching you. That's why we've also included an exercise or two at the end of most of the principles. These exercises have been designed to groom you for study success, and that's whether you're in year eight, starting university or just wanting to know how to learn better.

> Man's mind stretched to a new idea, never goes back to its original dimension.
> *- Oliver Wendell Holmes*

Incidentally Mr. Holmes seemed to "walk his talk", being adept at stretching minds. He once attended a meeting where he was the shortest man present.

"Dr Holmes," quipped a friend, I should think you'd feel rather small among us big fellows."

"I do," retorted Holmes. "I feel like a dime among a lot of pennies."

Stretching your mind is fun. It makes you a more interesting person. It will lead you to improved learning and better opportunities.

So how do you go about stretching your mind? The secret lies in first targeting a problem or challenge that lies in your way. It could be to lift your exam score in Science for instance. You then need to stretch your mind in two ways. First you need to brainstorm all the possible ways in which you could lift your exam score in Science. Second you need to stretch and flex your mind to achieve a rise in your exam score.

Let me give you another practical example. In the early 1990s when I didn't have enough money to go to University I began stretching my mind to think of all the ways in which I could raise that money. There was a problem and a challenge in my way. As I brainstormed and explored many different methods, I eventually hit on selling pizzas door to door. This may not work nowadays, but back then I sold pizzas to almost every second door I knocked on. Soon enough there was a team of us doing it. Through stretching your mind across different options, being determined and trying all the bases, the problem can be overcome and the challenge can be embraced.

To take another example, one student (let's call him Anthony) wanted to move up from "E" level to "A" or "B" level in his school. This was no easy task given that it is very rare for any student in his school to move up more than one level at a time. One of the problems facing Anthony was that his writing and level of general knowledge was below average. Like a good apple pie, the basics of apple and pastry were there, but the spices, flavours and ice cream were not. He needed extra knowledge and skill to move up the class levels in his school.

Anthony began a carefully designed reading programme designed to increase his level in writing and general knowledge. He moved from reading one randomly selected book per month, to at least one strategically selected book every week. He began keeping a reading journal constantly practicing his ability to write descriptive reviews of literature. He took an extra class in speechmaking to improve his confidence in his own expressive ability. Within three months Anthony had stretched his mind to a new dimension and a new operating level. He moved up to the "A" level shortly afterwards.

The importance of a regular and active reading diet will be emphasized again and again in this guide. Ordinary students have their minds stretched only at school. Top students have their minds stretched at school and in their leisure time. Apart from extra classes and conversations with people who know a lot more than you, the best way to stretch your mind in your leisure time is to read. Reading opens your mind to new opinions, new worlds and new possibilities. Through reading non-fiction books your mind is exposed to other people's findings and opinions. Through reading fiction books your mind is exposed to the complexities of characters and situations that make up stories.

There is always a special but unknown relationship between the reader and the writer. As the writer writes they befriend every imagined reader who might one day pick up their work. They draw those readers into their story or message. And as each reader replies in their own thoughts, there is a conversation of minds.

When you read, you think. When you think, your mind is stretched. Reading automatically engages the brain. At the same time reading becomes mind stretching and educational when you challenge what you read. For non-fiction books ask yourself if the writer's findings make logical sense. Ask if they are linked to examples and evidence. Ask if they are backed up by other writers and experts. For fiction books consider what it is, or is not, that makes the story believable and interesting, or unrealistic and pointless. If a stranger sat beside you on a bus and told you a story, in many cases you would challenge the story's truth or consider its point. Although written words are so often more carefully chosen, their truth should also be challenged by thinking people.

However, as valuable as reading books may be in stretching your mind, all the road maps in the world seem pointless if you don't know where you want to go.

Son, there is something else to watch out for.
There is no end to the writing of books, and too much study will wear you out.
- Ecclesiastes

No doubt Ecclesiastes was aware of the problem then, as now, that reading and studying by themselves without purpose can be very wearing. You read and study because you want to stretch your mind in order to be able to *do* something better. It is the *doing* that is most important. This is why in principle 5 we look at why it's important to relate what you study to life.

I tutored a boy from Asia once who spent his leisure time in many extra classes with tutors in subjects that ranged from English, to Speech, to Violin. Curious, I once asked the boy's mother why she enrolled him in so many programmes?

"So he can put food on the table when he grows old," she replied simply and practically.

It was at that moment that I realized this is one of the most important outcomes. "Food" in the mother's context could mean just that in terms of bread or rice, but it can also mean a comfortable house, a safe car or a good living.

A University graduate on average earns much more over their lifetime than a High school graduate, and there are many examples of how study success equates with later prosperity. But perhaps we all know of people who have made millions by dropping out of school and succeeding in business, sport or mass entertainment? In many such cases it would appear, that again, those individuals have been able to stretch their mind to find and exploit opportunities that have lead to their success.

Chance favours the prepared mind.
- Old proverb

The boy's mother understood that by ensuring her son's mind was stretched now, he would be better prepared to take advantage of chances that might come along in the future. And the future is becoming more competitive. There are so many students coming out of universities with advanced degrees. Competition for and within many jobs is intense. That means that although what we know and what grades we get are important, how we can adapt, create and dream our way into new and better things is probably a lot more important.

Of all the advantages which come to any young man, I believe it to be demonstrably true that poverty is the greatest.
- Joseph G. Holland

The theme of this book revolves around the idea of "where there is a will there is a way." To students and teachers alike, one of the main messages of this book is how to find the "will" both in yourself and in your students. Someone's will or motivation is a complex being. It has a life of its own. It is influenced by your past, present and sense of the future.

Two forces in life create a significant impact on success. One is the experience of going without, the other is the experience of having a high quality mentor to learn from. This is why so many of the world's most successful people seem to have experienced periods in their life where they have had to "go without" or where they have had to endure shortcomings and difficult struggles. At the same time, they have often looked to the success of others to model their own ambitions.

Studying for a career or more importantly for the extension and development of your own mind requires you to make efforts now for a better future. One great aspect of study that builds character, is that being a student requires a life of poverty. Students generally do not have a lot of money. They must study and learn in order to compete in tomorrow's world to make a living.

As a student I felt that my mind was most inventive and attuned to opportunities around me. At University I was learning from lecturers and tutors during the day. In what little spare time I had, I was trying to find ways to pay for my course fees and board. I set up a small tutoring company. To earn money from this I had to ensure that both my teaching and the tutors that I contracted were extremely good, otherwise I would have soon been out of business. I worked hard, but somehow there was always the energy and time to keep going and to keep extending myself. I would do a full day of university classes, then go and tutor high school students for most of the evening. Finally I ate a re-heated hostel dinner at 9pm of "spot the chicken", (which by this time tasted surprising good), then studied into the night. On the weekends my roommates and I would talk long into the night, comparing the subjects we were studying or just plain joking and gossiping. I loved what I was doing and somehow there was always more energy to do more. These tough years were among the most rewarding.

After I graduated, I continued developing various businesses. But soon enough life became comfortable. I relaxed. I tried all sorts of things that took my fancy. As life became easier, I lost some of the old hunger to succeed. And it took years to become aware that you can never stop learning and never stop pushing yourself if you want to reach self-fulfillment.

Exercise 1

Write down a problem or challenge you currently face. This problem or challenge should represent an obstacle that if you could overcome it, would greatly improve things for you. It could be your ability in some area or your performance in some subject. It could be not having enough money, friendship or time.

First, brainstorm all the ways in which you could overcome this problem or rise to this challenge. Write them down in a list. Be creative without limit: Add every possible idea that passes your mind to your list.

Second, consider this list of ideas you have formulated. Choose one of the best ideas and write down the process or programme that would allow you to use that idea to overcome your problem or obstacle.

Principle 2: Solve problems and answer questions

It's a sunny day and the grass has a brightness never seen in the town. It's the last day of our school camp. We are all in the field, each with our long bows and a number of arrows by our sides. The bull's-eye targets are lined up across the field. I pull back and fire. The arrow plunges aimlessly into the grass long before the target. With another scarce arrow I take another shot, this time with a dangerously long pull. The arrow flies into the sky, sails above the target and for a moment puts nearby grazing cattle at great risk. Mr. Smith, the supervising teaching gives me a "watch it buddy" sort of glare. This is harder than it looks. Success all depends on the *trajectory of the shot*.

The lesson of archery is similar to that of study success, as it is in other sports, business and in life. The trajectory of the shot is the key success factor. Trajectory depends on how you aim. It depends on how much you stretch the string of your bow. If you want to hit that bull's-eye without relying on the slim chances of luck, you must get the trajectory right.

In study success some of getting the trajectory right involves knowing where you're going and finding where your motivation or drive lies. This we will come to. Right now we're looking at stretching the string of your bow. This means learning to stretch and flex your mind as much as possible.

Principle 2 states that when you have a question that arouses your curiosity, a question that you want an answer for, you're going to be pushed to find a solution. You're going to be pushed to stretch enough to get the trajectory *just right*. Good teachers begin by arousing their students' curiosity. Curiosity helps to unlock creativity in students since it forces them to question, whether that involves questioning some aspect of life, or some part of a subject.

Where there's a will there's a way

I can feel the coins bulging and rattling in my pocket as I walk into the convenience store.

"Six packs of Star Wars bubble gum please" I tell the shopkeeper.

He raises his eyebrows with a smile. What does that mean? How should I know, I'm only eight years old.

As soon as I'm outside the store and in the backseat of my father's car I begin ripping open the packets. I don't care about the gum. It's the cards I want.

"Got this one, this one, this one and this one. I need Boba Fett the bounty hunter."

A week later after some serious trading, Jeremy, my best friend and I are approaching Krishna in the playground. His father owns a corner store. Maybe he could help us get some more Star Wars cards?

Back in those days Star Wars cards from bubble gum packs were big business. It's not Star Wars now, but if you had some of the rare numbers like Boba Fett you could do some serious trading. The point is that in our little eight-year-old minds we had a big probing question. That question was how to get the cards we needed to complete our collection and break the playground trading monopolies? One way was to make friends with Krishna whose dad owned the corner store. Another way was to visit stores all over town to try and find new cards.

Faced with something we really wanted, a problem and a question, it was surprising to see how resourceful we become as eight-year-old boys. But you don't see so much of this sort of determination, questioning and resourcefulness in our learning. Whether that is at school, high school or in tertiary studies.

> Life is a daring challenge or nothing.
> *- Helen Keller*

For study success you must apply this kind of energy and that type of challenge to your learning.

> Risk, risk everything.
> *- Katherine Mansfield*

Solving problems and answering questions is a golden way to stretch your mind. By rising to the challenge and through taking risks, problems are overcome and questions are answered. Let's take a look at some examples:

When Jason failed his practice English exam he had a problem on his hands.

But it was a problem, like most problems, that could be solved. His main problem was that he didn't understand Shakespeare. Whilst trying to read *Macbeth*, his eyes would drift to the sea view from his bedroom window. His mind would follow, thinking of his car, or his girlfriend or what sort of pizza he'd ask his dad to order for dinner.

But things changed when he saw *Macbeth* on video. He'd followed and understood the play completely. Then he'd watched it a second time, pausing the video to scribble down notes or a useful quote or two. It was almost like watching an action movie with his mates but he was actually studying for his exam.

That had been his problem, understanding Shakespeare. Fortunately, his father Chris had recognized that Jason was a visual person. That's why Jason was good at mathematics and science but lousy at English. He could see pictures and structures with numbers and diagrams but not with words. Chris had suggested that Jason get *Macbeth* on video. And that solved the problem for Jason of being unable to understand the play through the script alone. The actors performed the words and brought the play to life for him. That caught his interest. He went from dreading Shakespeare to enjoying it. He went from having nothing to write about the play in his exam essays to being a near expert.

The principle of solving problems and answering questions often leads to success where you least expect it. For instance, if you've ever eaten a salad from a Wendy's fast food restaurant, it is interesting to consider how Wendy's got into the salad business. And not only did they enter the salad business, they became one of the biggest sellers of salads amongst the major fast food chains. Dave Thomas, the founder of Wendy's was an entrepreneur. Entrepreneurs succeed by solving problems and answering questions they come up against in their businesses. You see, Wendy's never used to do salads. But they had this problem of wasting the "hearts" of the lettuces. To make their burgers they used the crisp outer leaves of the lettuce and were left with the centres, or the "hearts". The question was what to do with these "hearts" and how to find a profitable use for them. Those hearts were used to make the salads. The rest is history.

As you go through your academic life you'll come up against problems and questions. That's inevitable. It's not so much the problems and questions you come up against but how you deal with them. That's exactly what a good education prepares you for. That's exactly the approach you need to succeed in study. You need to know how to solve problems and answer questions whether they be related to writing, literature, mathematics or science.

Reading quality literature is a brilliant way to consider how problems are solved and questions are answered. As readers we relate to the dilemmas faced by the characters. Let's consider the novel *Of Mice and Men* by John Steinbeck for a moment, one of my favourites. This American classic has long been studied at the high school level, yet its meaning and message remains real to all ages.

Of Mice and Men is a story about two men set in the Salinas Valley of California during the Depression. It is as much a story of desperation and loneliness as it is the American dream. George and Lennie are two unlikely friends who travel across the vast countryside together seeking work on ranches. Typically they work on a ranch for a time, and then move on to the next one. Men such as these who work the ranches are usually lonely. The earn their money, they spend their money, they work, they move on. And that is their life, their lonely life.

Yet for George and Lennie it is different. That is because they have each other and because they have a shared dream. This is even more unusual given that the friendship between George and Lennie is a rare and unlikely one. While George is wily and clever, Lennie is simple to the point of mental disability. Lennie thinks and speaks slowly, not truly understanding how the world is. That's why when they walk along the road Lennie likes to collect pet mice and keep them in his pockets. He pets them, not realizing that in his big fingers they are soon squeezed to death.

From the opening scenes we see the contrast between George and Lennie. We come across George's quickness and restlessness as we do Lennie's size and heaviness of step. We also come across George's vision, which is the ideal that binds the two men together.

George recognizes the rarity of their friendship. He explains to Lennie many times that they are not like other men who work on ranches since they have each other to talk to. He explains that one day the pair of them will have a 'little place', a ranch of their own, and there they will raise animals and live off the land. This explanation fills Lennie with joy and excitement as he imagines himself tending the rabbits in an alfalfa patch. Yet the dreams of owning their own ranch are dependent on saving enough money first.

Of Mice and Men is brutally realistic. Just as it looks as though there is a way for the pair to have their ranch, Lennie is confronted with Curley's flirtatious wife. Curley is the boss's son and he is as aggressive as he is mean. Curley's wife is interested in Lennie. She likes him, especially since she's aware that he's recently crushed her husband's hand in a scuffle. She's sitting beside Lennie talking to him. And just then, as with the mice, and later with the puppies, Lennie wants to pat her soft dress. But he pats too hard and Curley's wife becomes scared. She starts to scream. At this, Lennie becomes scared and tries to silence her in his big hands lest he gets in trouble with George. So strong is Lennie that he doesn't know his own strength. He innocently kills Curely's wife as he did the puppy and the mice.

When George realizes what's happened, it is too late. He knows that Curley is going to come after Lennie to avenge both his wife's death and his broken hand and pride. George knows that when Curley finds Lennie, he's going to inflict a slow and painful death upon him. He knows that wherever they go, Curley and his men will hunt Lennie down.

Exercise 2

Write down very clearly an explanation of what you would do if you were in George's shoes. If you know the story well, and you know George's subsequent actions you may like to consider if you would have done the same thing in his position. Consider that the chance of escape in these times for a man so large and so simple is virtually impossible. Consider how George must confront Lennie and the alternative for Lennie in Curley's hands.

Read on only after you have written your explanation…

George's solution is tragic and final. Hiding in the bush Lennie is close to capture. George tells him one last time of their great dream to have their own ranch. He tells him one last time of the deep rarity of their friendship. And unseen by Lennie he pulls the trigger of his gun at the back of Lennie's head, killing the big man quickly and suddenly. In this way Lennie dies happy. He dies with the dream fresh in his mind, and in the ironic security of his deep friendship. For George, this seems the only way to spare Lennie from the pain Curley might inflict on him, and to ensure he leaves the world happy. George is then set to become just another lonely man who works on ranches. The reader is left to wonder whether the efforts of men are sometimes as pointlessly similar to those of mice.

In thinking about solving serious problems and finding answers you are stretching your mind. This is a life skill that will enable you to not only achieve study success but success in your chosen career.

Problem cases and stretching the mind

Life is full of problems and obstacles. It is the surmounting of such problems and obstacles that defines us, that demonstrates our determination and leads to the development of our abilities and skills. Problems force you to think, to solve, to figure out and ultimately to learn. In the next few exercises you'll be playing the role of a judge trying to figure out who is most responsible for a series of unfortunate events. You'll need to use your powers of clear thought and reasoning to answer certain questions and resolve the problems.

Exercise 3

The Elevator Case

Before beginning to consider this problem case you should write down four names: Norman, Jim, Mike and David.

Here's what happened: In the 1970s, down a busy street in a large city, a new hotel was being built from the remains of an old building. In fact by the time Norman walked down that street on a hot summer afternoon the hotel was almost complete, and the new building cut out an attractive entrance foyer into the street.

That day Norman was walking the sidewalk anxiously in search of a bathroom. He needed to find one, and urgently. The new hotel offered the promise of luxurious facilities, so he walked in the front door, entering the lobby.

Jim, working as a porter was first to meet Norman:

"I'm sorry sir, we're not open for business yet and don't expect to be until next month."

"Well, I was just wondering if I could use your bathroom. It's a bit of an emergency if you know what I mean?" replied Norman.

"In that case it's down the aisle, the second door on your left." Jim instructed.

Norman hurried off down the corridor, following the helpful porter's directions.

About ten minutes before Norman arrived at the hotel, Mike, an elevator serviceman had just left for his lunch break. That day he had been installing a new elevator as part of the refurbishments. He had left the empty shaft behind a closed door, waiting for the actual elevator to arrive. Since Mike knew he'd only be out for ten minutes to grab a sandwich and a coffee from the nearby lunch bar, he didn't leave any warning sign as to the empty hole awaiting the elevator.

Since Norman had entered the hotel, David, the hotel manager had been viewing his every movement on the new lobby security camera. As manager, it was his responsibility to ensure the security of the premises and in actual fact he should have immediately gone down to the lobby and asked what this guy was doing. But since he had his hands full with a cream cheese and avocado bagel, not to mention a cappuccino, he thought he'd just watch the man on video camera for a bit.

But David lost sight of Norman when he opened the door. And Norman walked quickly and purposefully into the bathroom, having held himself with some discomfort for what had seemed hours. However, Norman mistakenly failed to see the ground under him and he at once plunged into the dark hole that was the empty elevator shaft, plunging four levels down into the hard concrete of the car park below, which broke his neck on impact.

Mike returned from lunch to hear soft and pained cries for help from an agonizing voice echoing up the shaft...

Your task is to decide and explain logically who you think is most responsible for Norman's terrible accident. Was it Norman himself for not watching where he was going? Was it Jim for plainly giving the poor man the wrong directions? Was it Mike for leaving the empty elevator shaft unmarked and unattended? Was it David, who as manager of the hotel, ought to have been ultimately responsible for ensuring people did not walk in from the street to an unsafe environment.

Decide and explain your answer before turning the page and reading on...

This case was based on a similar legal case that went to court. The judge found that Mike was most responsible for Norman's injury since any reasonable person would have been able to foresee that if they left an empty elevator shaft exposed, and unmarked without any warning or danger sign, such an accident could occur, even though it was unlikely and remote. Mike was considered to have been careless, or "negligent".

The Theatre Case

Before beginning to consider this problem case you should write down five names: Hayden, Margot, Leo, Andy and Barry .

Hayden loves going to the theatre to watch live stage plays, and when he does he always makes sure he reserves a seat in the front two rows. On the night in question he arrived at the theatre for opening night of the play, having booked a seat in the front row. However, to his annoyance he found the first two rows were in fact roped off. There was a sign that said "please do not sit here."

Hayden ignored the sign, climbed under the rope and positioned himself strategically in the middle of the front row. The theatre manager on duty that night was Margot, who upon noticing Hayden sitting in the banned rows, immediately went over to confront him. However on the way over to him, an elderly member of the audience already seated asked Margot to show her where the bathroom was. Margot directed her and as she walked past the lobby she met an old friend of hers' she hadn't seen for many months. By the time they had finished their conversation the play had already started and Margot had absentmindedly forgotten about Hayden sitting in the front row where he shouldn't be.

The play was a Western. Leo was the lead actor and Andy the props manager. A few days earlier, Andy had approached his friend Barry for one of Leo's props - a small cowboy style revolver. Barry, who was a collector of guns gave Andy such a revolver without thinking too much more of it, knowing that it would probably be used somewhere in the upcoming play.

Andy did not check the gun, assuming that it would not be operational and handed it to Leo that night. Midway into the play, Leo performed a shoot-out scene, firing first toward the front of the stage at an imaginary villain approaching him on horseback. Unfortunately the gun was operational and fully loaded. The shot hit and injured Hayden.

Your task is to decide and explain logically who you think is most responsible for Hayden's terrible injury. Was it Hayden himself for sitting where he shouldn't be? Was it the theatre manager Margot, for failing to tell him to move before the play begun? Was it Leo for firing the shot? Was it Andy or Barry for failing to check and for supplying the working firearm?

Decide and explain your answer before turning the page and reading on…

This case was loosely based on another legal case that went to court. The judge found that Andy was most responsible for Hayden's injury since any reasonable person would have checked a potentially dangerous item such as a gun before using it in a stage play. Andy should have checked the gun to ensure that it was not loaded and would not harm any of the actors or audience. His failure to do this was considered careless or negligent, and this mistake was most closely linked to the resulting accident.

Principle 3: Find your motivational base or driving force

The top 5 percent of students know something about where they're going and why they're going there. Let's take a typical example. We'll call him David. David regularly scored 90 percent plus in his exams and assignments. You could say he was a high achiever. Part of the reason for the level that he was operating at, was that he knew what he wanted to do with his future. Even in year 9, David knew he wanted to be a doctor and to get into medical school he knew he needed top grades throughout. The beauty for David was that he had something to work towards. That was his motivational base or driving force.

Motivational bases run deep. They let you see what you're trying to conquer. They keep a vivid picture in the front of your mind of the destination you're trying to reach. And why you're trying to reach it.

A mountain climb

Having such a clear visual goal or sense of motivation reminds me of the time I was climbing Mt Taranaki, 2,518 meters to the summit. Let me first advise you that then, as now, I am no mineral-water-sipping gym junkie. Preferring a good book to a jog in the park any day, or an afternoon at the movies, than playing football, I was hardly primed for mountain climbing. Furthermore I was carrying up a stomach whose cravings had long sided with burgers and pizzas over fresh garden salads. But that's not the point.

There were times when I wanted to turn back. Times when I decided mountaintops were for the falling of snow, not the desperate scratching of human boots. Times when the sun bore hot on me. When globules of salty sweat stung my eyeballs. Times when for every three steps up the scoria, you would slip and slide down two.

Surprisingly I made it to the top. The view was worth it, and the sense of achievement was even more worth it. What had kept me going was the view of the beautiful mountaintop covered in snow. That could often be seen from wherever I was on the mountain during my climb. That view was my motivational base, my visual picture of where I was going. I knew that if I followed the path to it, I would reach it in the end. I just hadn't anticipated the path would be so steep or that in some places it would be non-existent. But you get that.

As with mountain climbing the motivational base of seeing where you want to go works in study to push you through the good, the bad and the ugly times of the climb. And make no mistake study is a climb. It takes a concerted effort. It takes determination. It takes passion to reach your learning destination.

That's how the top 5 per cent of students reach that level. Let's look at some motivational bases in study. These are some of the driving forces that motivate the top students:

One of the most difficult elements with motivational bases is that you cannot always see your destination or goal. Indeed, much of the time climbing Mt Taranaki you can't see the summit. You're in the bush. The angle's wrong. It's blocked by rocks, snow or cloud cover. In these cases you have to imagine the top. It's the same in study. So often when you're studying you can't see the end result. You can't see the entry into medical school, or the rewarding career as a Doctor for example. What has a single research assignment got to do with all of that?

Study, as with most things is a huge sum of many parts. Just like when you build a house you start with a plot of land, bricks, windows and thousands of individual materials, steps and processes before the finished project can be realized.

True learning requires the understanding that succeeding in one part, such as an essay or an assignment, or understanding a concept well, contributes to overall study success.

A good deal of learning, study success and finding your motivational base involves getting to know yourself.

Knowledge of anything is also knowledge of oneself

When you study and come to understand how the themes in a Shakespeare play are communicated or you get to know how to solve Quadratic equations, you're tapping something inside you, you're stretching inner talents and you're getting to know some part of yourself.

When you take learning from the perspective that you're getting to know yourself, you're exploring and expanding your mind, you'll find a powerful motivational drive. Students who achieve in that top 5% have a strong motivational drive. We're going to be looking at where your drive to succeed comes from in study, because that is the fuel that keeps you studying and leads you to success. We're going to explore what drives you in your studies. Maybe now, if you're not the most driven student you can think about and discover a motivational base to begin from. That's what this programme is about. Your trajectory, your aim, knowing how to pull the string on your bow and where to aim is the important starting point.

First, to explore this large and overused word, "motivation": As selling things is to a business, motivation is to the student. Those students who score in the top 5 percent have a strong motivational base. You can see this through watching top students, average students and students who struggle. But the precise motivational base or drive is not always instant or easy to see. As we look at various motivational bases you might like to not only consider your drive and base, but that of your friends and other students. In saying this, beware of friends who succeed in exams and tell you that they never really study. It's more often than not a lie, and it reflects their strong need, their motivational base or their drive to compete.

In the boys' school I went to, competition was an important motivational base for many of the students. We would all be queuing outside the classroom ready to take the exam. And there would always be a handful of the most comfortable and smug students leaning against the classroom wall as if it were all just a game of golf.

"Haven't done any study for this one," they would casually boast.

A week later, when the scores came out they had *cleaned up*. In actual fact they'd done so much study they'd been so comfortable on the day their dishonesty was nothing but a satisfied bluster. That's why they were so comfortable. Study is a lot like an exercise regime for the mind. Just like an amateur boxer who's spent months getting fit and primed, he feels a lot more comfortable immediately before the match.

There were of course those students who said they hadn't studied at all. And they really hadn't. They were the ones who always looked as though they were facing yet another academic funeral. That happened to me once in a Computer Science course at University. I hated it. My motivation on a scale of one to ten was negative four. I wanted out of the paper. Suffice to say the three-hour exam was torture. I felt as though I had arrived in another country where everything was in a foreign language.

As for this important concept of motivation, an early study of it can be traced back to Abraham Maslow, who in 1955 came up with "The Hierarchy of Needs". Maslow said that human beings are motivated first by survival (having food, clothing and shelter), then security (the need to feel safe), then affiliation (the need to have friends and family to talk to and share things with), then self-esteem (the need to feel good about yourself) and finally self-fulfillment – the point of reaching your absolute potential. It was once estimated that only 5 percent of the population ever reach this level of self-fulfillment.

A lot of students fail to realize that study is not just about survival. As we discussed before, when you learn about anything you learn about yourself. As we study and learn we improve self-esteem. We become individuals who are more confident in ourselves, who understand others and who understand our world better. That makes us happier and better able to deal with everything in life that comes our way, from disappointment to decisions.

Beyond self-esteem, study presents the real opportunity for self-fulfillment. This means that when we study something we're interested in, that matches our talents and abilities, we reach the ability to be the best. From this an enormous sense of fulfillment can be gained.

Motivational bases/driving forces

The top 5 percent of students who routinely gain A's, reach a level of excellence and are operating at the 90 percent plus level, are usually driven by one or more of the following motivational bases:

1. Fulfillment from learning

Students gain a sense of drive and motivation because they enjoy what they're learning. They enjoy expanding their mind and their knowledge of themselves as they learn. Think about a subject or activity that you've really enjoyed learning. It's just been a pure pleasure, a walk in the park. Now you're motivated to learn that subject or activity because you enjoy it and get fulfillment from it.

2. Competition

Competition is an important driving force and motivational base. People are motivated to drive a faster car, participate in the most extreme sports, win prizes, trophies and the admiration of others. Top students get into the best courses at the best universities. They get the best jobs. They earn more money in the future. That on average is a fact. Yes, aiming to the best is a powerful motivational base.

To give you an example of this, a student, we'll call Paul, is typically the top scoring student in exams at his school for his year group. If he's not number one, he's in the top three. Paul is motivated to be number one. He's motivated toward study success because he fights for the number one position at his level.

Competition was a powerful motivator for me when I was at school. I began as student number two hundred or so in my year group and through a desire to compete and stretch myself I became one of the top students in English.

3. Teaching

Teaching is a powerful motivator. Good teaching develops student's creativity because it unlocks their sense of wonder. For many students a good teacher inspires them to learn. Consider the message in the movie *Dead Poets Society* starring Robin Williams as charismatic teacher, John Keating. Keating positively changes the beliefs of his students forever.

You may not instantly like every teacher you have. It takes a skilled student to find the best ways to learn from every different teacher's instruction style. For instance, a teacher who discusses ideas at length in class may need students who can spend a lot of their own time going through the additional exercises and explanations in the textbook. A teacher who provides notes and exercises in class may need students who can invest in plenty of their own general interest reading and thinking outside the classroom to inject the material with life.

4. Fear of failure

Fear of failure is a major motivator. It's a driving force since students are afraid to fail. They're afraid of not making the grade. Motivational expert Anthony Robbins says that all human beings are motivated by the desire to gain pleasure and the desire to avoid pain. He states that when we associate something with pain, we'll avoid it, and when we associate something with pleasure, we'll chase it. Students associate failure with pain. They associate failure with having to repeat the class, meaning a big waste of time and possibly the worry of their parents. Some students associate study success with pleasure. They associate learning with stretching their minds. They associate succeeding with praise and feelings of happiness and satisfaction. These students find it easier to achieve study success.

5. The beauty of knowledge

The beauty of knowledge and the sense that tasks can be done with beauty is a motivator and driving force for students, especially for those who are artistic. Some students experience beauty in writing a story, solving a mathematics puzzle or designing the layout of an assignment. Becoming aware of the fact that jobs can be done beautifully and through such beauty pleasure can be gained, is in itself a driving force. You can sharpen your sense of beauty by being alert to experience, being ready to change your ideas, and being open to inner feelings along with constant study and practice.

6. Future goals

Future goals are an important motivator. Some students are motivated by long term desires to enter a certain career or profession which requires an academic basis, or to simply have the confidence in their later life that comes from succeeding in school.

7. Following a system

The discipline and organization that comes with following a system or working within a structure is a motivational base or driving force for some students. These students like working within school and assessment systems. They enjoy organizing their notes and completing set tasks in an efficient manner. They like a sense of order, of answering questions and getting results in a structured setting.

8. Inspiration

Inspiration is a motivating force. It occurs when what you're learning excites your senses and imagination, like a wind surfer who catches a good breeze and a fine wave just at the perfect point.

9. Opportunity for creativity and self-expression

The opportunity to exercise your creativity and to express yourself is a powerful motivator. In learning new things and completing essays and assignments there's the opportunity to create your own ideas.

10. Being different or having the edge

Some students like to be different from others. They are motivated by learning and knowing things others do not. Some students are interested in researching into subjects so they have knowledge and an edge that sets them apart. These students are individuals who like to stand out.

11. Family and friends

Joseph, an old student I coached many years ago, and today a friend of mine, recently shared with me his dramatic transformation toward study success. Joseph lacked direction in his studies for some time. In high school he smoked cigarettes and dyed his jet-black hair blond. His friends around him weren't "study focused".

Joseph says that a lot of teenagers don't realize what the real world is like because they live in a sheltered environment provided for them by their families. For instance most teenagers don't have to worry about earning money and putting food on the table, that's done by their parents. Sometimes it's just not enough to know they have to succeed in school at that moment. Yet things changed for Joseph when he awakened to the real world and joined a new set of friends at Engineering School.

A combination of the motivational bases

One day I asked Joseph to do some work for me in my consulting company as a small part time job. At that time Joseph wondered why the going rate for his time was barely a fifth of the consulting rate we charged. He realized that it was because consultants had the qualifications to be able to convince clients to give them the work. The consultant could charge the premium rate because they could prove they had the knowledge required by the client. Those who did not have any qualifications could only get the going rate for their skills.

Joseph was aware however of the many business success stories of people whom begun with nothing but become extremely rich through taking risks and working hard in business. Yet he also wisely realized that these cases are rare when you look at the whole population. For most people, qualifications in this society give them an advantage in gaining a better rate of pay and thus a higher standard of living.

Joseph also considered a future as a musician. He thought playing the guitar could be his future. He practiced four hours a day and nearly failed year 12. He broke a school record with one of the lowest grades ever. By that stage he'd worked out how hard it was to ever make a good living from playing the guitar.

Things changed as Joseph begun to consider his future. He wanted a decent lifestyle. He wanted the respect that comes with a good job along with the time and money to engage his other passions such as playing the electric guitar. When he realized that to get this lifestyle in the future, he would have to study now, he cut his hair, quit smoking and began to focus.

A few years ago he entered the Engineering School at a highly respected tertiary institution. This led to even greater and more rapid changes for Joseph. He recently told me that "one thing that keeps me focused now, is that my self-esteem and competitiveness have awakened when I got into Engineering. People just compete with each other. They do anything they can to win." He's reached an advanced level now and says "I help out others unconditionally, but they ignore me when I'm in need, so it just makes me even more focused because I want to kick their butt so badly."

Joseph also gains motivation not only from his new group of friends in the Engineering School but also from his goals for the future. Enjoying Engineering, he has also realized he's the sort of guy who likes to help other people. His ultimate goal is to go on and study medicine, gaining a position in the future where he can integrate technology (his engineering) with medicine. This may mean study overseas and a substantial investment in his education, but it is an investment that will pay off. More importantly his driving forces of a likeminded group of friends, competition, enjoyment, interest and goals for the future provide a huge amount of personal satisfaction along the way.

The motivational bases

There are more motivational bases, some very particular to your own case. It is important to consider that motivation and drive are mental. Our motivational bases are usually unconscious, which means we aren't naturally or strongly aware of them. As we are motivated to eat due to hunger and to make friends due to loneliness we need to be motivated to achieve study success due to the need for a brighter future. That's why it's important to spend a few moments now thinking about where your motivation might come from, how to manage it and how to focus it for your study success. True motivation requires focus and just as we saw during the mountain climb, a visual sense of where you're going.

A man is what he thinks about all day long.
- *Ralph Waldo Emerson*

Exercise 4

Following is a list of the motivational bases. Add a couple more of your own to the list. Give yourself a score out of 10 as to how much you think these driving forces NOW motivate you.

When you have done that give yourself a score out of 10 as to how much you could easily motivate yourself if you focused on these driving forces, even if you don't believe you're already strongly motivated by them now.

When you've finished, add up the scores to give a total out of 20 and then multiply each by 5. You've now got a weighted percentile rank on the strength of driving forces and motivational bases that you can use to push yourself toward study success:

Motivational bases/driving forces

1. Fulfillment from learning
2. Competition
3. Teaching
4. Fear of failure
5. The beauty of knowledge
6. Future goals
7. Following a system
8. Inspiration
9. Opportunity for creativity and self-expression
10. Being different or having the edge
11. Family and friends
12. Your own personal motivational bases…

Part II: A plan for the future and a focus

Principle 4: Do each part well

In Part I we talked about stretching your mind, answering questions, solving problems and finding your motivational base. The most important thing to take from this is that it doesn't matter how you're doing now, that in believing in yourself, in the untapped potential of your mind, you can, and you will succeed in study. For a start you're already part of a special group of people who have picked this programme off the shelf. You've got the will to do your very best in learning, and where there's a will there's a way.

People who write books about how to do something really, really well want to help you. However, one thing that annoys me with many such books is that they don't go far enough. They give you the broad brushstrokes, the outline, the basic ideas. But you need the detail. You need the how. In this section we'll not only be looking at outline concepts such as stretching your mind or finding your motivation, we'll be looking at the specifics and the "how to". Things you can get to work on immediately.

People learn from people, like stone sharpens stone. I don't claim to know everything about learning success, but I've taught enough students over the years, and made enough mistakes myself to know that you have to do each part well. This is principle 4, and it's the hardest principle of all. In today's world of the Internet, global business and global brands, you're competing not only with the student sitting in the desk next to you, but ultimately with students all around the world.

How does this work? How can I make such a claim? Ultimately if you want to succeed at a world-class level, you have to do world-class work. Why aim for anything less? A top sports team doesn't just aim to beat the local club, it has to compete on a worldwide stage. An Olympic athlete won't get far by coming first in the school athletics, he or she has to take on the best the world has. If you consider the world of school, learning and study as the Olympics you begin to understand this viewpoint.

Years ago as a teenager I learnt the piano. I confess I was hopeless. My parents were finally convinced that I should give up when a music teacher said to them I didn't have much talent for it. Knowing what I know now, I could have been a good pianist. The trouble was that I didn't exercise principle 4. Do each part well. From its absence I learnt its importance.

For those of you who learn a musical instrument, you will know that music requires dedicated focus. It requires perfection. It requires a real attention to every detail in the music, from the mood, to the feeling, to in my case, actually hitting the right notes!

Now, you can probably guess what Principle 4, doing each part well, means for study success. It means doing every test, every exam, every assignment and participating in every school class as though your future counted on it, because in many ways it does.

So how to you do every part well? You need to enjoy the journey. You need to try and find some enjoyment and a sense of focus in each part. That means in every lesson, every essay, every assignment, you need to be able to find a way to enjoy the work, to immerse yourself deep into it, the way you would your favourite movie, book or computer game.

Imagine for a moment the journey of writing a book. It may never get published, even if it does, it may barely cover its costs. Yet if you focused on that while you were putting it together, the result would be hopeless. On the other hand if you focused on your message, your ideas and what you wanted to show or teach others, you may have something worthwhile at the end. You may even have a best seller.

In my Internet education book, *Click & Grow Rich,* I quoted from a successful teacher and leader of our time, a man who helped to change the course of history. Winston Churchill once described writing a book as swimming a river. Churchill talked about the stimulating and pleasant feeling of wading in feet, ankles and waist deep and then making an eager strike toward the opposite shore. As you reach the centre the river can be colder than first anticipated and the current can suddenly become dangerously swift. In the middle of the river there is a strong sentiment to give it all up and swim back to the safety of the shore just left. It is then that you realize it is just as far to the opposite shore but as you keep swimming, you reach what Churchill called the "middle of the middle", a harrowing no man's land of fear, frustration and despair. Summoning up final reserves of strength and determination you reach the opposite shore. By this time you are so bedraggled not to care much of what happens afterward. It is on reaching the shore that you are heralded with a success beyond what you hoped for. Looking back it is this journey of learning and courage that etches richness on your life. This is exactly why those who have achieved great success will tell you time and time again, it is the journey and not the view that makes it all worthwhile.

Now, don't get me wrong, I'm not asking you to write a book or swim a river. Remember any programme of study is made up of doing problems, answering questions, writing essays, solving equations or understanding classes. If you take the attitude of enjoying each small journey not as someone just waiting for it to finish, but as an explorer, you will meet with results beyond your wildest dreams. I have seen this occur before in the study of English literature when all of a sudden a student finds a literary text that they really like. Suddenly the essays they write about this text become filled with feeling and brilliance.

Okay, this all sounds promising, but what if my journey is not through some beautiful river? What if it's just hard, long, boring, and it's a struggle just to get through it?

Well, if you've chosen such a path and you feel that way, you may need to consider your choice - we'll de dealing with that soon in principle 7. But first, in your learning journey, here are some tips to get you through these hard times:

First, during any journey, you can't always see the end result. When you're writing those creative stories, you can't see yourself becoming someone brilliantly able to express yourself just yet. When you're working those chemistry problems, you can't see yourself entering the medical school just yet. When you're working those accounting problems, you can't see yourself owning that business just yet. But the sum of many small parts done well, leads to the great final result. Or in other words a good journey leads to a great view. In Part I we talked a bit about climbing a mountain. Most of the time you can't see the summit, you can't see your goal, but you keep climbing because you have the faith that your efforts now will lead to something. Not just the view from the top, but the valuable learning experience of the journey.

Stephen King, arguably the world's greatest thriller and horror writer, in his days starting out as a writer, once said of his efforts "I began to have long talks with myself at night about whether or not I was chasing a fool's dream." Again, it required faith in doing each part well, in writing each story well, to finally reach the top of his genre.

Principle 4, doing each part well requires not only the challenge of not always being able to see or visualize your end result, but being prepared to invest in something now to get a superior result in the future. That means what you learn from your classes, the problems you work, the essays you write or the assignments you complete at the moment will lift you to a higher place in the future. With more knowledge, better thinking and an improved ability to learn, not only will you find more opportunities in life, you'll find yourself thinking smarter and understanding more about yourself. As we learned in Part I, knowledge of anything is also knowledge of oneself.

Delayed gratification

The concept of being able to sacrifice and invest now for the future is known as delayed gratification. A very informative study of delayed gratification can be found in Daniel Goleman's book, *Emotional Intelligence*.

To explain the study and its results in a nutshell, imagine for a moment you are four years old. An instructor says to you that if you wait until he returns from running an errand you can have two marshmallows. If you don't want to wait, you can still have a marshmallow now but you can only have one. For a four year old this is a very tough dilemma.

What do you think you would have chosen at the age of four, considering one marshmallow was already placed in front on you while the instructor went to do his errand? Some of the four-year olds in the study were able to wait out the fifteen minutes or so that the instructor was away. Do remember that when you are four, fifteen minutes is a long time.

The four year olds who decided to wait it out tried all sorts of tricks and techniques to get them through. They talked to themselves, they covered their eyes so they couldn't see the marshmallow or some of them even attempted to sleep. Other children were more impulsive. They grabbed the one marshmallow in front of them and enjoyed themselves soon after the experimenter left.

Twelve to fourteen years later these very same children of the marshmallow survey were tested again upon graduating from high school. Now teenagers, the researchers wanted to see whether the early study on delayed gratification had any links to their attitudes, behavior and development now.

Interestingly those four years olds who had waited for that second marshmallow and delayed gratification were showing similar qualities many years later as teenagers. They were effective young people who had most of the skills necessary to deal with the stresses and strains of life. Just as principle 4 says to do each part well, this very group, over a decade later, was able to concentrate on doing something well now, no matter how difficult, so they could get a better result in the future.

So what about that group of four year olds who couldn't wait and downed the first marshmallow upon the instructor leaving the room? This group was very different. They were more likely to be shy, stubborn and easily upset or frustrated. They were more likely to be short tempered and impulsive. Just as they did so many years ago, they wanted everything now. As before, they were less successful because they had not learned to delay gratification and invest or sacrifice now for a better result in the future.

The lesson remains in principle 4, to do each part well you have to sacrifice and invest now, you have to deal with the hardship now of each part of your study in order to succeed in the future. You have to be prepared to continue up that steep hill even when you can't see the top just yet.

Rod Stewart, an extraordinarily successful rock singer, in an interview for the *60 Minutes* show remarked that to be a successful musician you have to live and breathe music. You can't just pick up a guitar at the end of the day and expect to hit the big time. Doing something really well requires focus. Just like a magnifying glass harnessing the suns rays to burn-up a piece of paper, you need to hone your learning skills to achieve study success.

One of the secrets of doing each part well, and one that the top 5 percent of students use, is that they are able to find joy and interest in their subjects and in each part, whether that be an essay, an assignment or a sequence of problems. Bill Gates, supposedly one of the world's richest men, provides a superb example of this approach in *The Max Strategy*, a book by Dale Dauten. Gates admits it's a fluke he's so rich. He insists that he was never motivated by money. He was motivated by the idea that "computers are neat."

Employing one of the key strategies of leading motivational expert, Tony Robbins, we need to learn to remove pain and associate pleasure with activities that can lead to our success. You need to find pleasure in your study, in each part of it. In this area the power of focus is paramount. If you focus on the great things in each of your subjects, you will come to associate pleasure with study and your academic life will become a whole lot easier.

Exercise 5

List the subjects you are currently studying in your school or tertiary institution. Next to each one write down what you enjoy about studying these subjects. Here's some examples quoted from top students to get you started:

On English: "I love learning to find new ways to express myself and my ideas in words that create beautiful and clear meanings."

On Mathematics: "You can actually have a lot of fun stretching your mind in new dimensions to solve complex problems and puzzles. It's really good to see what mathematics can do to your mind."

On Science: "To know how the world around us works and to be able to explain it is the most important and interesting thing."

On History: "Some of the best stories are true, and happened in the past. Learning from these stories we can understand more about our world today, where it comes from and where it's going."

On Economics: "I can learn about how to earn more money in my future, by understanding the laws of economics."

Now add your own quotes. What do you find enjoyable about the subjects you currently study?

Whenever you don't feel like doing your very best in some part of study for one of these subjects you can turn back to this exercise and remind yourself of what it is that catches your interest in each of your subjects. Then focus on that pleasure, rather than the pain.

By now, you've gained an understanding of the important principle of doing everything well. If you want to succeed in the world and compete with the world, everything you do has to be world-class. Remember, doing each part well involves stretching your mind, solving problems and answering questions, being motivated and then giving each and every part your very best efforts. Surprisingly most students don't give each part their best efforts. They just try to get it done on time and out of the way. Think about how you approach your own studies. Are you giving each part everything or just enough to get through it?

To give you a little practice on doing each part well, we're going to look at the process of developing something and then polishing it to perfection. In doing anything well, it is through the polish that the shine is gained. Let's consider William Shakespeare for a moment. Today he is regarded as one of the greatest playwrights the English language produced. Much of the reason for this is that his work is of such high quality that it is as relevant today as it was hundreds of years ago. It has stood the test of time.

To be a great playwright you must understand the human heart and be able to show that through characters and their speech. Shakespeare had such polish since his work succeeded in showing real human hearts, from the depression of Hamlet, to the young love of Romeo, to the old pride of Lear and to the fierce ambition of Macbeth.

Exercise 6

In this next exercise, we're going to be looking at some great lines from Shakespeare's "As you Like It."

Your task is to rewrite these lines to see if you can first, edit "The Seven Ages of Man" to better reflect modern life, and second, to inject the flow of the language with your very own style.

The Seven Ages of Man
from *As You Like It*

By William Shakespeare

All the world's a stage,
And all the men and women merely players:
They have their exits and their entrances;
And one man in his time plays many parts,
His acts being seven ages. At first the infant,
Mewling and puking in the nurse's arms.
And then the whining school-boy, with his satchel,
And shining morning face, creeping like snail
Unwilling to school. And then the lover,
Sighing like furnace with a woeful ballad
Made to his mistress' eyebrow. Then a soldier
Full of strange oaths, and bearded like the pard,
Jealous in honour, sudden and quick in quarrel,
Seeking the bubble reputation
Even in the cannon's mouth. And then the justice,
In fair round belly with good capon lin'd,
With eyes severe and beard of formal cut,
Full of wise sayings and modern instances;
And so he plays his part. This sixth age shifts
Into the lean and slipper'd pantaloon,
With spectacles on his nose and pouch on side,
His youthful hose well saved, a world to wide
For his shrunk shank; and his big manly voice,
Turning again toward childish treble, pipes
And whistles in his sound. Last scene of all,
That ends this strange eventful history,
Is second childishness and mere oblivion,
Sans* teeth, sans eyes, sans taste, sans everything.

*Sans means without

Principle 5: Relate it to life

Education must become co-extensive with life

You can learn anything faster and better if you use it and do it. Accelerated learning is learning by doing. An important part of learning by doing is imagining how each part of your studies relates to the real world. Following principle 4, doing each part well, you can then take this a step further with principle 5: relate each part to the real world.

Learning is also a force that goes beyond school. Today's world requires life-long learning. Tomorrow's world will require life-long accelerated learning. All learning begins with a need or a question. In school there is the need to pass and move on to the next stage. Yet this is not always the best kind of learning since many students don't understand why the need to do well is so important. A better form of learning is the question. When you want to find out the answer to something or solve a problem your learning is more *motivated*. The mind thrives on curiosity and the search for answers. This force in learning can be applied in school, in the workplace and in business. Turn what you need to know into questions and then make these questions the targets for your study.

Take the example of Paula (not her real name), a school student struggling in creative writing. In a class of thirty students it was sometimes difficult to get an exact understanding of just what it is that makes a great story. Paula wasn't getting great marks in the writing sections in tests nor for her essays. She had a question that was affecting her life: "What is it exactly that makes a great story". Searching on the Internet she found twenty five rules for great writing. They were posted on the web site of a literary agent who arranged the sale of manuscripts to publishers. Some of those manuscripts had become best selling novels. Paula practiced applying the twenty five rules. She was soon scoring the best for creative writing work in her class.

> Education must become co-extensive with life.
> - *Gandhi*

What does Gandhi's famous line above mean? It means that everything we learn must be applied to improve the way we live. Now this comes back to what we learned before: Knowledge and understanding of anything is knowledge and understanding of yourself. Here you are learning the principles that the top 5 percent of students in our schools and tertiary institutions follow. However when you learn anything, the true test of how much you will advance depends on how much you apply it.

Let's look at an example of how learning and applying even one principle can totally change your life. Remember, applying what you learn in your life is key. You can learn the principles of the top students, however you will only get the results if you remember and apply these principles as the top students do.

Now for that example: It was once reported that highly paid comedian Jerry Seinfeld earned enough interest on his interest to live on for the rest of his life. Seinfeld had his lucky breaks such as getting on the *Tonight Show* and being picked up for television. However, Seinfeld actively practiced a principle that according to a recent biography, he picked up from a young age. That principle was the power of rehearsal. Many less successful stand up comedians working the difficult, sometimes humiliating and often unpaid circuit of comedy clubs didn't put into practice this principle to the extent that Jerry Seinfeld did. They knew the principle of the power of rehearsal, a standard principle for dramatic arts such as stand up comedy, but they didn't rehearse to the degree of Seinfeld who would live and breathe his routines, going over and over them until they were perfectly timed.

The reason why most students don't succeed is that they don't practice enough. You learn by doing, that means practicing. And practicing takes time. You get good at writing English essays by writing more essays. You get good at solving mathematics puzzles by solving more puzzles.

Now as you write an essay for example, you can apply it to the real world, you can apply it to life, by imagining that for every word you write and every sentence you construct, you're improving your ability to write and express things, a power that will give you advantages throughout your life. On that subject, think for a moment when you apply for a job, or develop a business plan to set up a business, the quality of how you write and express yourself may mean the difference between success and failure. Seinfeld seemed to succeed because he had faith that with superior rehearsal he would be a superior comic. With superior practice and application you have the ability to become skilled in any field you choose.

The principle of relating learning to life is a powerful one.

To learn is not merely to accumulate data; it is to rebuild one's world
- Robert Grudin

When you begin to see learning as rebuilding your world, you start to understand why great world leaders such as Gandhi said that education must become co-extensive to life.

The limiting force

In exercising the first five principles of stretching your mind, solving problems and answering questions, finding your motivational base, doing each part well and relating it to life, there is one force that limits the potential of all of these.

That very force is explained most elegantly in the first verse of Robert Herrick's poem, To Virgins to Make Much of Time:

Gather ye rosebuds while ye may,
Old Time is still a-flying;
And this same flower that smiles today,
To-morrow will be dying.

Time waits for no one. And in applying principle 5 of relating learning to life, managing time becomes most important. Top students understand something about education and life being co-extensive, since they see learning as a natural part of life, as is eating, sleeping and breathing.

Top students don't seem to watch a lot of TV. Perhaps one of the reasons for this is that television, despite what people think, is not a great way to learn. But why not you ask? Surely when you're watching TV you're absorbing information? That's exactly it, you're *absorbing* information, you're not doing anything with that information. On the other hand when you read a book or attend a class your mind is involved, your mind is working and doing things, activating your learning muscles.

For example when you read a novel your mind must direct the movie, paint the sets, select the actors and choose the settings. Every time you read a work of fiction, a multi-million dollar movie is being made inside your mind. That's why one mind is more powerful than all the directors, actors and exotic locations of ten Hollywood blockbusters. When you read, you're expanding your mind to new ideas, and as we learnt in principle 1, your mind stretched to a new idea, never goes back to its original dimension.

Part of managing your time to learn and study means seizing time. The old Latin maxim is "carpe diem", which means to seize the day. It's easy to waste time by not doing anything productive. Seizing time means using every moment to learn, think and stretch your mind. One significant difference between top students and bottom to average students is that top students seem to use their leisure time to participate in activities that stretch their minds such as reading or socializing that involves active debate and discussion.

Although I hate to say it, sport can also be a factor that crowds out important learning time for students. There are many arguments that suggest sport improves mental development as well as leadership and social skills, but to date there is no proof that participation in sports has a positive relationship with academic results. In fact excessive participation in sports may have a negative relationship with academic results.

Of course, sports are an essential part of a child's growth, and no school should ignore its duty to develop children's bodies as well as their minds, but, it is ten times, a hundred times more important for schools to expand the scope of our children's mental abilities than to break records in athletic events.
- *Toru Kumon as interviewed by David Russell*

Understanding that time develops or devours everything, is important in understanding why learning must be a part of your day to day life to achieve study success. All students are given similar amounts of time to learn similar principles, yet some experience accelerated learning while others do just enough to survive. It is better to succeed than to survive. Survival by itself is unrewarding.

In the next exercise we're going to be looking at a real world problem. You're going to be using and combining skills from various areas to solve that problem. But more importantly, whether you find solving the problem simple or easy, depending on your level, you're going to understand the importance of applying learning to the real world.

Exercise 7

Imagine for a moment that a mountain biking club has organized a competition day, and you've won the opportunity to sell bottled mineral water throughout the day.
- Let's assume there's going to be 500 people involved and on a fine day they will buy 200 bottles of water when each product is $1. The elasticity* is such that for a 10 cent increase in price, quantity purchased will drop by 20 (or rise by 20 for a 10 cent decrease in price), until $1.50 after which nobody will buy.

- All prices must be set in 10c units such as 90c, $1, $1.10 etc to minimize the need to carry spare change.
- From the wholesaler you buy a bottle of mineral water for 30c.
- You need to buy ice to keep the water cool. Approximately 1kg of ice is required for every 50 units at the cost of $3 per kg.
- You need to purchase a blackboard sign to promote what you're selling at the cost of $10.
- You have already agreed to donate $30 to the club equipment fund.

*Elasticity measures how responsive customers are to price changes

Now, here's where it gets tricky… The day before you will need to check the weather forecast and set a price to advertise… there's 2 possible scenarios:

1. On a fine day, the demand and ice requirements will be as above.
2. On an overcast day the demand for water will drop to 150 bottles at $1, and for a 10 cent increase in price, quantity purchased will fall by 25 (or rise by 25 for a 10 cent decrease in price). However only 1 kg of ice will be required for every 100 units of product. The club has agreed to reduce the donation to $20 on an overcast day.

Your task is to make as much money for yourself as possible. For each of the 2 weather scenarios calculate the best selling price and write the best possible advertisement for your sign.

Notes: Readers with more experience in mathematics and economics will find this easier as they will be able to design formulae, however, through trial and error other readers should be able to find an answer for each scenario. More importantly you're exercising some of our earlier principles of stretching your mind, solving problems, finding motivation, doing each part well and now principle 5, relating what you learn to life in the real world.

Principle 6: Learn from failure

It's okay to fail the first time. But our education system treats failure badly. Which is a pity since it's the best way to learn anything. Take for example, a student who has just received a failure grade in an English exam. They received that failure grade because they had poor exam technique and didn't know how to structure short essay answers. Some students would take that failure result as some form of lasting tattoo that identifies them as being poor in the subject of English for the rest of their life. All that really happened was they needed a bit more work. With the right practice and the humble ability to learn from failure, all students can succeed in study.

The biggest failure is the failure to learn from failure. That's because you learn more from failing than you do from succeeding. That student who has just failed the English exam can now learn that they didn't have their exam or essay technique right. They can now start working on this to improve. They can get better marks. Careful learning from failure can help to lift them toward the top 5% of students. That's because a student who fails actually has the opportunity to learn more than a student who succeeds. But only if they are open.

In theory this should mean that it's harder to stay at the top than it is to reach the top. That's seldom the case though, because most students don't seem to learn from their failings, instead letting their failings get them down. The more questions you fail, the more opportunity you have to learn. But we're not saying that failure is completely good. If you consistently failed you wouldn't get anywhere in study of any kind. It would be a certain route to flunking. But it is normal for students to fail in some areas during their learning lives. These failures are not failures at all. They are learning opportunities.

The mentality of learning from failure

Most people are successful because they don't give up. Persistence pays off. That's because persistence puts you first in line in terms of both skill and luck. When you persist and persist you develop your skill. Because you keep trying so many times, eventually luck is going to smile on you.

When success in school or business or in any pursuit does come it looks instant and easy. That's seldom the case. You have to realize the effort and persistence that has been invested behind the scenes. It is the same with the top students. They aim and practice to reach a level of excellence. The idea that you can learn from failure and become a "success in failure" is a popular teaching in the area of business start-ups. These teachings can to some extent be applied in study to help you achieve good results. Study is like business. It requires effort, the acquiring of skill and the ability to learn new things.

Let's take an example from the business world on "becoming a success at failure". A story that is hard to beat and something of a legend in the business of television infomercial marketing is that of Suzanne Paul. In *Success in Business*, Paul Smith tells her story:

Suzanne's early life took place in a poor, working class area of England. She suffered poverty, once remarking that when the souls of her shoes wore through they were replaced with cardboard. When she left school to work in retail, she began keeping notebooks of various plans and business ideas. Her friends and family would often ask her what her next plan was and she would tell them. The trouble is that most of her plans never worked. She would have to return to her job as a store assistant.

When she left England for New Zealand she was about to try business plan 40. Remember, this is after 39 other plans had failed. She was 35 years old. If Plan 40 had failed she would have had to go back to her family in England and tell them she was right back where she had started – with nothing. Yet she also reasoned that she had failed so many times before, that she would just have to pick herself up and start all over again if it didn't work. Plan 40 was in fact the television infomercial marketing for the Natural Glow cosmetics product. Did Suzanne fail in Plan 40? I am happy to tell you that from these persistent beginnings she built a multi-million dollar business employing many people.

This attitude of learning by failing and being prepared to give everything a try is an attitude required for study success. Learning is an ongoing series of tests and experiments. You can't succeed without trying, and trying will involve making mistakes and learning from those mistakes to gain the best results.

Dale Dauten in *The Max Strategy* describes this attitude in a rule he prescribes for success: the rule simply is "experiments never fail". Winston Churchill once described success as the ability to go from one failure to another with no loss of enthusiasm. "I've never failed at anything in my life" he said, "I was simply given another opportunity to get it right." This is why principle 6 is to learn from failure.

In school English one of my first exam results was 41 per cent. Fortunately a good teacher told me that the problem was with my essay technique and I could learn a lot from my poor result. Afterwards I went on to gain a scholarship in English and am now in the process of writing my third book.

Principle 6 says that the top 5 per cent of students succeed in study because they learn from failure.

Exercise 8

For a moment think about 4 major failures you can recall in your learning.

Every student has their failures, because there isn't a student that gets 100 per cent in everything all the time. Now write down your failures.

Okay, beside each failure write down the gold, what you learnt from this failure.

Principle 7: Focus for results

The Hawthorne Effect

Imagine for a moment that you work in the factory for a major electronics company. In the late 1920s The General Electric Company wanted to sell more light bulbs, so along with other electronics companies, it supported studies on the relationship between lighting and productivity (which is how quickly the workers produce products). The studies began like most scientific experiments with a test group and a control group. The level of lighting was gradually increased for the test group and was not changed for the control group.

Imagine for a moment that your work in the factory is being monitored to see if either (a) an increase in lighting will increase your performance or whether (b) an increase in lighting will have no effect on your performance. Whether you're in the test group or control group, you're likely to perform better. That's exactly what happened in the studies. It was found that people singled out for a study might improve their performance because of the added attention they receive from the researchers, rather than because of any specific factors being tested.

This is known as the Hawthorne effect, named after the Hawthorne plant of the Western Electric Company where the studies were first conducted. In the science of management this lead to increased interest in how human relations affected worker performance.

So what is the lesson from the Hawthorne Effect and principle 7 - with focus comes results?

Students who achieve at the highest levels focus on their subjects. More importantly I've noticed they usually receive focused attention on their studies from other people, which may include their parents or competitive friends. The lessons here are fourfold.

First, students themselves must focus on studies as if they are completing the most important ongoing learning experiment of their lives.

Second, students should look to join tuition classes and form their own study groups with friends to share the problems and experiences of learning and studying and to gain something of the Hawthorne effect: The feeling that they are not alone, that others are on the same mission and care about the destination they are all aiming to reach together.

Third, there are important lessons for parents and teachers. To achieve the improved study results, as the Hawthorne effect did for productivity in factories, it is important to give attention to students' results.

Fourth, society needs to celebrate academic success and the media needs to show the importance of studying for future success. It pays to keep in mind that a student studying diligently alone does not make good television, but the intelligence and skills they go on to use certainly does. We see heroes benefit from years of study but forget the importance of that preparation.

> The deepest principle in human nature is the craving to be appreciated.
> *- William Jones*

For teenagers you can multiply the force of this statement by three.

The trouble for so many students is that they so often work very hard in school and tertiary institutions, with the only reward being their grades. To gain something of a Hawthorne effect students need to appreciate the true meaning of great results and in turn gain appreciation from the people around them.

One student gained some of the best results in a top performing school. We'll call him Andrew. He gained a strong Hawthorne effect from his father. And that mostly seemed to happen in the car: His father drove him and his siblings all over the city for sports matches, after school tuition and weekend shopping. In the car Andrew and his father discussed Andrew's study successes and failings. His father was like a sports coach keeping a promising young player at the top of his game.

All students are promising young players with the right focus.

Focus is a mindset. One of the hardest things for many students is to sit for long periods of time concentrating on learning a subject or process. Study doesn't always have to be sitting at a desk quietly. Learning can be active. You can form a group with friends to discuss a subject. You can study outside. You can record notes on to audiocassettes to listen for memorization. You can draw up a timetable of study times and keep a record of how many hours studied for rewards in the form of breaks.

Jessica used to keep a record of all the hours she spent studying. She really enjoyed shopping for new clothes. Every hour of study earned her a dollar added to her shopping budget. After fifty to a hundred hours she had the chance to go out and buy herself a new outfit.

In the following principles we're going to be looking at the specific techniques you can use for achieving focus and flow in study over a variety of core subjects. For the meantime the point in principle 7 is that attention and focus on study both by you and through interacting with others is a vital factor in study success.

Principle 8: Make a plan for the future

Principle 8 is based on the finding that many of the students who achieve top results have a plan. A plan doesn't have to be an exact goal as to your future career. In some cases it can be, in other cases it may be just a sense of direction. Basically a plan is a picture in your mind of the direction you want to follow. Life doesn't always go to plan. Many people go through career changes. But plans along the way help to direct focus and increase motivation.

At the same time look at the changes in the world around you. Leaders in developed countries are appealing to businesses and educators to embrace the "knowledge economy". This really means that the wealth of a country is becoming more and more related to the new and clever ideas it can produce rather than simply making and selling goods and services that we already know about. It means that the future success of a country depends more on the ideas in people's minds than the pastures that feed cattle or the factories that turn cotton into clothes. That's because the world is becoming globalised. Globalisation means that because of the Internet, communications technology and increased free trade, the world is becoming one place. Most goods and services will probably be made wherever they can be produced most cheaply. But be sure their special concept, brand and design will come from the cleverest people in the most knowledge advanced countries. And it is the concept, the brand and the design that creates the most wealth. That's why knowledge is king.

There is an old saying that life is what happens to you while you're making other plans. But what happens to you has something to do with the plans you make. Plans help define and direct the actions you take. And there are two kinds of people, people who do things and people who don't. In a short space of time life separates those who do things from those who do not. Those who do things get what they want. Those who do not buy lottery tickets. It is in getting things done that you might gain some success and satisfaction. As a successful businessman once said, "know what you want and then keep learning, keep trying and one of these days you might profit."

Men of action are favored by The Goddess of Good Luck.
George S. Clason

Always remember what you have learnt. Your education is your life
– guard it well.
- Proverbs

Along the same lines it pays to remember that the aim of education and study is not just to get a job or know enough about some field to turn it into a business. Many of the jobs that will exist in tomorrow's "knowledge economy" we don't even know about today. Twenty years ago who would have even known about software development jobs, corporate life coaches or e-commerce consultants?

One of the most important aims of study and education is to improve your mind and yourself. Knowledge of anything is knowledge of oneself. Knowledge of anything gives the mind increased flexibility to adapt to the rapidly changing world of the "knowledge-based society".

The purpose of education is to train the mind and to teach it how to think.
- Aristotle

The only way to have real job security in the future, to get a good job with a growing income, is to have real skills and the ability to learn new ones.
- President Clinton, 1994 State of the Union Address

Study helps you develop real skills and teaches you the ability to learn new ones. It is important to keep in mind that experience is the most important way to develop skills. That's why we've been emphasizing in all principles that applying learning to the real

world and learning by doing is extremely important. Beyond this your career direction gives your education meaning and purpose. It helps set the stage for the play you are writing.

So how do you go about making a plan for the future? The level of detail required in your plan obviously depends on your year of study.

If you've already embarked on tertiary studies you should have a clear idea of the career direction you're heading.

If you're in year 12-13 you should have a clear idea of the different career options you may wish to pursue.

If you're in year 9-11 you should have some idea of the different career options that interest you.

And finally if you're in year 7 & 8 you should know about some different career options that are out there and might be of interest to you.

Deciding on a career direction is a three-step decision process:

First you must have a good understanding of yourself. As we know, this understanding comes from learning. Knowledge of anything is knowledge of oneself. If for example your favorite subject is accounting, the accountancy profession may be a career direction worth considering.

Second you need to learn about different careers that may interest you. You need to find out the key factors required for success. For example if you want to be an architect, seek out people working in that profession and ask them what the job is like in terms of training required, difficulty level, earnings, highlights and lowlights. Try to be objective in such analysis. People's feelings for their job can be dependent on all sorts of factors ranging from the company they work for to the degree of success they have been able to reach in their career. It is a good idea to collect together a scrapbook of information, articles and advertisements for different jobs.

Third you need to carefully consider the best match of your individual traits and abilities with the characteristics of each career. This means you need to consider how well suited you think you would be to a career over the long run based on your knowledge of yourself, your likes, your dislikes and personality.

When discussing career options many students say they don't know, because they don't know themselves, what they're good at, or what they're like. The only way to really know what something is like and how well suited you are at it, is to do it. If for instance you really dislike the subject of accounting now, and you dislike completing journals and trial balances, chances are you may not enjoy it as a job. If you don't know what you like, the answer is to study more, to study different things and to try different activities until you gain more knowledge of yourself. For instance, David (whom we met in principle 3) knew he wanted to be a doctor when he began studying and practicing for a first aid certificate. He already loved science, and that additional learning and practical exposure helped him to realize he also had the need to help people.

Tomorrow's world is one of competitive career choices. It has been estimated more and more of the workforce will be self-employed. You need skills and knowledge but more than ever you need to be able to learn new skills and adapt the ones you have.

One simple rule is go to university. Over a lifetime studies show that college graduates earn on average much, much more than those who only graduate from high school.

Even if you're still only in year 9, start saving now. A part time job, so long as it doesn't take up too many study hours can be a good thing. When you work you do things and you learn about how businesses operate and what it's like to work, even if you're only flipping burgers. I put myself through university in part by tutoring high school students, and I sometimes think I learnt twice as much teaching as I did studying myself.

Exercise 9

Career options brainstorming

List 17 career areas that you know of or interest you. They could be anything from a physiotherapist to a wine maker. Make the list without limits! This exercise is intended to get you thinking about the way you feel about career choices and directions. It is to assist you in thinking about and forming your own plans. Now when you've completed that list, give each career a score out of 10 as to how much it really interests you. Second give the career a score out of 10 as to how good you think you might be at it. Finally give the career a score out of 10 as to its prospects and its income levels. Total each out of 30. You now have a ranked and weighted idea of some career options it may be worth you pursuing.

Past experience

Another side to consider in career planning is to analyse what you have already done in terms of subjects, activities or jobs. In this exercise you will list subjects, activities or jobs you have experienced in your recent past. You will then give each a score out of 10 for "enjoyment" (how much you liked the subject), "degree of talent" (the extent to which the work came 'naturally' to you) and "prospects" (the potential to make a worthwhile career from this subject).

For example, take Paul, a year 12 student:

	Enjoyment	Talent	Prospects	
School subjects:				
1. English	8	8	6	/ 22
2. Mathematics	4	3	7	/ 14
3. Accounting	6	5	8	/ 19
4. Economics	7	6	7	/ 20
5. History	7	7	5	/ 19
Other activities:				
1. Piano lessons	5	3	3	/ 11
2. Computer trouble-shooting	8	7	8	/ 23
3. Golf	9	2	2	/ 13

Paul's analysis would suggest that he is well suited to a career involving computers, business subjects and English writing. Alongside brainstorming of relevant career areas in exercise 9, this analysis can also be considered to assist in career planning.

Principle 9: Gain total self-confidence in studies

Principle 9 is based on the finding that the top 5 per cent of students succeed in study because they're more confident. They're confident that even if they fail, they'll learn from their failings and do better next time. They're confident that given any question or problem they can stretch their mind to find a way of tackling it and an answer. They're confident because of their drive and motivation. They're confident that they will do each part well. They're confident that what they're doing relates to the real world. They're confident of their focus and they're confident of their plans for the future.

Remember in learning everyone has a different style. There are no right or wrong ways.

There are 3 rules for writing a novel, unfortunately no one knows what they are.
- Somerset Maugham

By the 1930s Somerset Maugham was the world's highest paid writer. In the same way there are no fixed rules for learning. The only certain rule is that many students tend to underestimate their abilities. At the same time parents and even some teachers underestimate student's abilities. When a student finds a new world to explore they also find untapped potential to learn. And when a student begins to tap that potential and he or she begins to learn, then confidence grows. That's because knowledge of any subject leads to knowledge of oneself. Knowledge of oneself leads to improved self esteem and confidence.

Every child is a "gifted" child in ways we normally do not appreciate.
- Toru Kumon

Toru Kumon is the father of the well regarded "Kumon" method of mathematics education that builds confidence through a progressive step by step programme. Mr. Kumon was inspired to begin the development of a learning programme when his son, then in a Japanese elementary school, was experiencing problems in mathematics. As a teacher, Kumon recalled his days as a student when he was introduced to *jigaku-jishuu* "self-study and self-learning", Using this method he developed confidence in mathematics. He passed this on to his son and later to students worldwide who would come to study the "Kumon Method". Self-study and self-learning works to build your confidence as a student when you study difficult things and *master* them, or raise searching questions and *answer* them, or pose challenging problems and *solve* them.

It is our job as educators, not to stuff knowledge into children as if they were merely empty boxes, but to encourage each individual child to want to learn, to enjoy learning and to be capable of studying whatever they need to or wish to in the future.

- Toru Kumon interviewed by David Russell

With effort and determination every student can find their way to perform at the top. You can enjoy learning and become capable to study whatever you need to or wish to. Be prepared to stretch your mind (principle 1). You can practice this by solving problems and answering questions, especially difficult ones (principle 2). Be hungry for knowledge and know something about the driving forces that make you want to learn (principle 3). Become a perfectionist who does everything so well that your work gives you pride and satisfaction (principle 4).

Remember that almost all learning is related to life in the world. The more you know and the more skills you have, the better equipped you will be to guide yourself through life, whether that be in finding work, overcoming obstacles or feeling good about yourself (principle 5). Don't be put off by failure. Things don't always work the first time, or the second. But when you learn from the times you fall, on the third time you are three times as likely to succeed (principle 6). In all of this you have to be able to sit still, to discipline yourself, to focus, to concentrate and to gain that sense of flow in studies that comes with finding a challenge to stretch your mind (principle 7). Know something about where you want to go and what you want out of life. This will help give you the drive to succeed. (principle 8). And finally in this section on drive and focus, know that you have the mind of a genius waiting to be unlocked. You have the key and every time you open the door you become stronger and more confident (principle 9).

Remember the more you study, the more you learn and the more you exercise these principles the more confident you will become as a student. When you experience total self-confidence in your studies, learning, achievement and success will flow.

Yet how do you stay confident? How do you stay motivated? This is a problem to solve in itself. Students find different methods. The important thing is to find a method. One day in a class I asked Jamie, a top performing student, about this chain he always wears around his neck under his *Mossimo* sweaters.

"Why do you always wear that?" I asked him, out of pure curiosity more than anything else.

"Well, it gives me confidence" came the reply from the artistic teenager.

"Confidence?" I queried.

"Yeah, my grandmother gave me this chain. She's dead now. But she always wanted me to do well in school. So this is my confidence chain. When I wear it, it reminds me that every moment is valuable and to learn all I can with the time I got."

In Part III we're going to be looking at some specific tools and techniques for study success.

Intelligent people are always eager and ready to learn. Getting wisdom is the most important thing you can do. Whatever else you get, get insight. To the person with insight, it is all clear. To the well informed it is all plain. You will become wise and your knowledge will give you pleasure.
- Proverbs

Part III: Accelerated learning and improved memory

Principle 10: Leap the obstacles

How do you learn more, how do you learn faster and how do you enjoy it? Researching this area for the guide was maddening. I spent hours reading books on accelerated learning. Many of them said very similar things. The practicality of many of the techniques was questionable. "Learn by doing", "use subliminal music", "do exercises", "stretch", "listen to music in your sleep", "turn your science notes into nursery rhymes" some said. Hang on, I thought, few students want to do all these strange exercises. They just want to learn.

In this section we're going to be looking at the basics. It was once said that all you need to learn is a teacher, a student and a log to sit on. This goes back to the earlier message that people sharpen people like stone sharpens stone. Good teaching stems from the logic and practicality of knowledge itself. If you want to know where a glass of milk comes from, you start with a cow.

Before you begin planting learning seeds of success, you need to weed the garden. Consider, what are the main things that slow down your learning? What holds you back from learning as much as you could and getting even better results? What decelerates your learning instead of accelerates it?

First, let's have a look at a number of factors that experience and research combined tend to suggest are common complaints for students:

1. "This is so boring, it just doesn't interest me."

2. "This is too hard, I don't understand any of it."

3. "I'm no good at this subject."

4. "The teacher is hopeless, I can't understand what they're saying."

5. "I don't like this subject."

6. "I've got too many other things on to do this properly."

Success in anything involves finding a way to leap the obstacles that would hold you back. This is why some people succeed and others don't when it comes to the crunch point. Obstacles confound some, yet spur on others to greater heights of performance. For a moment, let's look at how you can leap the mental and attitudinal obstacles just mentioned.

1. "You find the subject boring."

D. H Lawrence once said "if it doesn't absorb you, if it isn't any fun, don't do it." In some cases this is good advice. If, however, no matter what you try, you just don't find a specific subject interesting, perhaps the headlines are clear: Don't plan a career of further studies or work specializing in this subject. It will drive you crazy.

On the other hand, pain is part of gain. If you get past the surface layer of boredom and frustration, you can find a well of interest in most subjects.

The trick to finding any subject interesting goes back to principles 1-5, stretching your mind, solving problems and answering questions, finding driving forces, doing each part well and relating it to life.

So, when you're bored with a subject, and you just do not think it is "you", begin by finding ways to stretch your mind through solving problems and answering questions. Work on your driving forces. If you're motivated by being different, go a bit further and see if you can find out interesting parts of your subject that nobody else knows, even your teacher. Most importantly of all, you still need to do this subject well to reach study success, to be a top student. You will find the motivation to do the subject well if you *relate it to life*.

To relate a subject to life, answer the following questions:
What job or function does this subject explain?
How can working with this subject's problems expand my mind?
What can this subject teach me about myself and my abilities?
Do I know anyone who works with this subject?
How could this subject be useful to my future?

2. "This is too hard, I don't understand any of it."

If you've tried everything, you've read all the notes and you cannot, you absolutely cannot figure it out by yourself, don't be afraid to ask for help. Ask your teacher, classmates or ideally a good tutor. Don't brush it aside. So many students fail because they don't ask when they know they need help, they just move on. *Do not move on.* Find a solution, gain understanding and invest the extra time to practice and memorize. Moving on without solving the problem is like walking from a car accident scene leaving someone to die, when they didn't need to.

> Students learn in school between nine and four, but it is the study and motivation they achieve out of school that leads to study success.
> - *Accelerated Learning Institute (www.acceleratedlearn.com)*

3. "I'm no good at this subject."

Some students learn in different ways from others. We'll be looking at this in principle 14. Yet all students have the ability to learn and become good in any subject with patience and practice. Make a goal to become good at your worst subject.

> You must do the thing you think you cannot do.
> - *Eleanor Roosevelt*

Your most difficult subject represents your tallest mountain, and the higher the climb, the better the view and the more you will learn and experience along the way. Turning your bad subjects into good subjects is the ultimate challenge. It is a challenge that the top students rise to.

4. "The teacher is hopeless, I can't understand what they're saying."

> Over the piano was printed a notice: please do not shoot the pianist. He is doing his best.
> - *Oscar Wilde*

The responsibility for your learning ultimately rests with you. The most successful learners and thinkers throughout history, learners like Aristotle and Einstein, have largely taught themselves. You must learn to explore, to search materials in libraries, to read and to form your own ideas in every subject and in every part of every subject.

> The greatest talent is the ability to strip a theory until the simple basic idea emerges with clarity.
> - *Albert Einstein*

Finding that basic idea, that basic clarity, as it did for Einstein, comes down to the learner, not the teacher.

5. "I don't like this subject."

The main reason students don't like a subject is that they don't see themselves in this subject. They don't see the subject as being of interest to them or part of them or of any relevance to their life.

> Set me a task in which I can put something of myself, and it is a task no longer; it is a joy, it is art.
> *- Bliss Carmen*

If you want to succeed in a subject, you can't go around hating it. It's a bit like expecting you and your boyfriend or girlfriend to have a great relationship when you dislike each other. As with people you have to look for the good and fine things. You have to look for the interesting parts in a subject, for the interesting applications to life or to your future, for the way it stretches your mind and ultimately how you can put yourself into it.

A student of mine, we'll call him Wayne, hated high school English literature. He was a superb mathematician, scoring nearly 100% in that subject. Yet when it came to English, he struggled to get over 50%. You see Wayne had an analytical mind, he liked to deal with numbers and puzzles. Discussing the themes in the play King Lear, or analyzing the observations in the poetry of Robert Frost was a complete waste of time as far as he was concerned.

What Wayne didn't know was how much the subject of English literature had been waiting for him. Waiting for him like a long lost friend. You see, once Wayne realized that his brilliant analytical and mathematical mind could be stretched to consider and explain the problems in the literary texts, he suddenly began to own them, to take the works on as his, as he would a series of mathematics problems. He began to realize that the same logic and problem solving abilities could be applied to literature. He began to realize that as with showing workings in mathematics problems, he could show his thoughts through the vocabulary of language to explain problems and issues in literature. Instead of going around thinking that essay writing to him was like a fish trying to ride a bicycle, he began to realize that essay writing was really just the explanation of the solving of a big puzzle.

> Be the change you are trying to create.
> *- Gandhi*

This means you must embrace the subjects you hate. As with Wayne and his road to success in the subject of English, you have to throw yourself into the subject to conquer it's slopes of difficulty.

6. "I've got too many other things to do to do this properly."

Study, as with holding down a job or running a business requires organization. Students need to be organized. You need to have a system in place to cope with the workload, especially as it grows during exam time. The trick to managing workload is to plan, prioritise and do one thing at a time. That process begins by making a plan of what has to be completed or studied for upcoming tests, assignments and for ongoing revision. The best plan is one that from the beginning of the year to the end of the year is everyday and ongoing. Study is one hundred times easier when you keep up with the material on a daily basis rather than having to cram at test time. A typical study plan should aim to revise and update notes daily. Assignment completion and test revision should take priority as they come up. A study timetable is highly recommended as this makes study a part of your regular routine, over time making the process much easier.

Different subjects will require varying amounts of study to reach your best possible level. That's because different subjects call on different skills. Most students find some subjects easier than others. But with concentrated study on weak areas, they can be turned into strong areas in the fullness of time. Top students are those who can adapt and *stretch* their minds to perform in all subject areas.

The best moments usually occur when a person's body or mind is stretched to its limits in a voluntary effort to accomplish something difficult and worthwhile.
- Mihaly Csiksezentmihalyi

Accomplishing success in all your subjects is something difficult but extraordinarily worthwhile. When you stretch your abilities to this extent, you build learning muscles that will help you achieve learning and study success throughout your life.

Principle 10 is leap the obstacles.

If at first you don't succeed, something is blocking your way.
- Michael Ray

Just as you train a horse to show jump you train your mind to believe all obstacles can be leaped, and in time, you train it how. But more on show jumping coming up in principle 11...

Exercise 10

Write down the five biggest obstacles you currently face on one half of a page. On the other side write down what you will do to overcome this obstacle based on the teachings in principle 10.

Principle 11: Show off your skill

One of Beethoven's most well known pieces is his beautiful and haunting Moonlight Sonata. He was deeply in love with the 17-year-old Countess Giulietta Guicciardi, and dedicated the piece to her. It could be said that he wrote the piece to impress her, to show off to her, to win her love. It was, as we will see again in a moment, showmanship.

The sonata got its name when poet Ludwig Rellstab described the music as being "like moonlight shining on a lake" in 1832. Yet it is unlikely that Beethoven would accept that.

Although audiences were initially disturbed by the power of this work, Beethoven was soon complaining about its popularity: "Surely I've written better things," he once wrote.

This piece remains a crowd-puller in concert halls all over the world, and has been used in many other places, such as the movies *Misery* and *Crimson Tide*; Cindy and Saffron's *Past, Present and Future*; and, supposedly, backwards in the Beatles' "Because".

A friend of mine once told me a story about a brief meeting he had with Salvador Dali many years ago. Dali was considered to be one of the most impressive artists of the twentieth century. Meeting him in a square, he told the great artist he had traveled thousands of miles to ask him a question, "how did he become one of the world's great painters?"

Apparently a stylishly dressed Dali walked with him a little toward the sea and replied that the secret of such success was showmanship.

The desire to demonstrate skill can be seen in many successful efforts. When Wellington hosted the Lord of the Rings trilogy movie, *The Return of the King*, movie history was made. The New Zealand Herald reported "few films have been greeted with more excitement – a mix of national pride and movie star adulation – or such numbers." Yet all of this begun with enterprising New Zealand director, Peter Jackson who simply wanted to make great films from his home town and convinced people that he could by demonstrating his skill through film making. Jackson made the kind of films that he wanted to see, and in doing so insisted on exacting levels of quality.

> Do something so well that people will pay to see you do it again.
> *- Walt Disney*

"Showing off" skills is something some top students naturally seem to enjoy doing. In writing an essay top students show off the level of skill they have developed in language expression, or the level of knowledge they have of a text. In mathematics or computer science they show off their skill to solve difficult problems and the "extra for experts" bonus sections. In science, history or geography, they show off their knowledge and interpretations.

Just like a magician earns the respect of his audience by showing off his best tricks first and last, so does a student earn respect from teachers, their peers and ultimately themselves by showing off their skill and knowledge.

A student I taught, Kevin (not his real name) happens to be one of the best mathematicians in his class. He once told me that he enjoys showing off his skill, because other students envy him and want him to teach them. It gives him a position of power and recognition. And that is not an unpleasant position to be in when you're a 15 year-old guy.

Exercise 11

In this exercise it is your chance to show off your skill. If you're good at writing, produce a page of poetry or prose. If you're good at mathematics, set up a problem and show the solution. If you're good at art, draw a picture or diagram. If you're a scientist, create a brief working drawing for an invention.

Principle 12: Access a river of flow

In principle 10 we looked at leaping obstacles and in principle 11, we looked at showing off your skill. Yet for many students the real questions are "how do I get totally involved in my studies? How do I find them interesting? How do I get absorbed to reach my very best level?"

Top students are able to reach a level of involvement in their studies other students do not. This comes from the fact that they are inspired by what they're learning.

At such a moment whatever you are doing no longer requires as much effort. It's like a cyclist catching a tail wind, or a canoeist finding the main channel of a river.

Think for a moment about a time when you've totally enjoyed something so much that it has become effortless. What was it that made you forget everything else and become totally absorbed?

The most likely explanation is that there was a real opportunity to put something of yourself into the work. There was the opportunity to do the work your way.

Cherish forever what makes you unique, 'cuz you're really a yawn if it goes!
- Bette Midler

Achieving flow is not only a mental experience. It is also a whole body experience. The best learning isn't just made of thinking about things in your mind, it's made of feeling them in your body. Feeling what you learn and learning by doing are important principles in accelerated learning and super learning.

> Great ideas originate in the muscles.
> *- Thomas Edison*

For example, when you're writing about a text, you need to feel the meaning of the text, and the emotions of the writer or the characters. Before you can begin to reach flow, you must get to work. The top students succeed because on average, they work much harder and they study longer than other students.

> Whatever you can do or dream you can do, begin it. Boldness has genius, power and magic to it.
> *- Geothe*

The need to study more and begin earlier can readily be seen in the remarkable performance of Asian students in American schools. In recent times Asian Americans on average have performed better in school than caucasions. The reason for this comes down to studying more, working harder and getting started earlier.

A review by a Stanford sociologist, Sanford Dorenbusch found that Asian-Americans spent 40 percent more time doing homework than other students. The findings included the theme that whilst American parents tended to accept a child's weaker areas and focus on the strengths, the attitude for Asians seemed to be that if you're not achieving you study later at night and if you're still not achieving you wake up earlier and study in the morning. Asian parents seemed to believe that anyone can do well in school with the right effort, and in many ways this fact alone seems to point to the academic success of Asian students in the United States, Canada, Australia and New Zealand.

Achieving a state of flow

Flow is a state where you forget yourself. It is the opposite of worry. Instead of being lost in nervous worry, students in states of flow are so absorbed in the task at hand that they stop worrying about daily life, grades and even doing well. Students who perform at their peak while in a state of flow are not worried about how they are doing. They are not concerned with thoughts of success or failure. It is the pleasure of what they are doing that motivates them.

At times when people throughout history have outdone their own abilities, or achieved something that appears superhuman, this state of flow has been involved. Being able to enter this flow is one of the greatest skills to master. You harness all your emotions for the service of performance and learning. Students who experience flow often say later that they "got on a high".

So once you have started, once you are prepared to put the work in, how do you get into a state of flow? The first step is to concentrate. A highly concentrated state is the essence of flow. It takes some effort to reach this level of concentration but once locked in, the flow becomes a force itself, the task becomes effortless and other worries disappear.

The second step to enter flow is to choose a challenge within whatever you are doing that is neither too easy nor too difficult. If the task is too easy for you, you will become bored. If it is too difficult, or there is too much to do, you can become frustrated and anxious. Every task is made up of parts. You need to select each part to challenge you. Flow involves finding the crest of the wave, the flow of the river or that tiny mountain path between the two valleys of boredom and anxiety. Traveling that path with concerted effort will lead to an unexpected success.

Studies have found that students who achieve their potential and beyond are drawn to learning because it puts them in a state of flow. To achieve such flow you need to be motivated from the inside rather than by any promise or reward. You learn best when you have something you care about and can get pleasure from being involved in.

Flow requires a level of complete concentration. To achieve that level of concentration you must *feel* what you are doing, not only thinking it in the mind, but feeling it in the muscles. To feel what you are learning you must see, hear, say and do. To learn more and reach a state of flow you should use as many of your senses as possible during the task at hand.

For example, when I write I sometimes like to listen to classical music. This is not for everyone, but the music relaxes me, sharpens my concentration and gives a rhythm to my typing. At times I imagine my computer keyboard is a piano keyboard. I try to visualize, to see what I am typing. I try to imagine how what I am typing will affect the people who read it or hear it. And occasionally, only occasionally one may experience moments where words flow effortlessly, and the usual hard slog of research and writing is suddenly a summer breeze.

To use all your senses in learning, you must also use your sense of fantasy to imagine how learning stimulates each sense. Fantasy itself is important in flow as you disappear into another world that your learning creates, a more exciting, beautiful or terrifying world.

When I examined myself and my methods of thought, I came to the conclusion that the gift of fantasy has meant more to me than my talent for absorbing positive knowledge.
- *Albert Einstein*

Exercise 12

Record three activities, tasks or times in which you have experienced a state of flow. Record each activity, the state of flow and then how any or all of your senses were activated.

Principle 13: Harness the magic of memory

Our ability to remember something well rests on 3 principles: repetition, interest and association. As we use our memory it becomes more powerful.

> The memory strengthens as you lay burdens upon it and becomes trustworthy as you trust it.
> - *Thomas De Quincey*

The memory is also like other parts of the body. It is stronger under adrenalin. Under pressure the memory performs better. Imagine for a moment you were facing a firing squad and whether you lived or died depended on your memory. Chances are under such circumstances your memory would flex into action as a very powerful tool.

But how do top students use their memory to achieve study success and what can you do to improve your memory now? Inside this principle we're going to be looking at some hot tips and techniques to get your memory functioning with the capacity of the highly adaptable and finely engineered machine that it really is.

A recent CNN report announced a Harvard Medical School study that found that sleep helps improve memory. The report, led by assistant professor of psychiatry Robert Stickgold found that people who slept after learning and practicing a new task remembered more about it the next day than people who stayed up all night after learning the same thing. According to Stickgold "it seems that memories normally wash out of the brain unless some process nails them down."

Human beings have extremely good memories. They hold more information than the most powerful of computers. Yet human memories have a filing system that at first seems illogical. That's because memory works on the basis of association. If, for example I say to you the word "airplane", you remember a number of factors by association, such as what an airplane looks like, the different sorts of airplanes, the feeling of an airplane ride if you have experienced that, airplane take-offs, landings and the airports to which they arrive and leave. Also by association you ought to be able to name numerous international airline companies such as Air New Zealand or Qantas thanks to brand building advertising campaigns that wash across our television screens. And perhaps your association could easily stretch to the marketing messages carried by the brands of such Airlines. "Singapore Girl, A Great Way to Fly" for example, was the slogan of Singapore Airlines.

We can learn a lot from the practices of the marketing industry. Marketers know that our memories work by association and that is why they seek to create pleasant and interesting associations for their brands that are repeated with advertising frequency. Marketers know that the cradle of human memory is rooted in repetition, interest and association.

Now, if memory is an animal that works best by association, to harness the magic of our memories we need to learn to use it by association. Suppose for instance you are wanting to learn a quote from the play, King Lear by William Shakespeare. The quote is one said by Gloucester in his darker hours:

"As flies to wanton boys are we to the Gods, they kill us for their sport."

To simply remember the string of words is a difficult process. To create in our minds a picture of boys killing flies creates a visual association that is much easier to remember.

Alternatively if we were memorizing the steps involved to complete a mathematics problem or accounting statement, we could create acronym associations to assist us.

Acronym associations use letters that create sometimes odd, but usually memorable words such as ROYGBIV to remember the colors of the rainbow. ROYGBIV stands for Red, Orange, Yellow, Green, Blue, Indigo, Violet: The colours of the rainbow.

When you start forming strong picture associations you'll be surprised at how quickly and easily you can remember things. Finding ways to harness the magic of memory and exercising such methods becomes extremely useful when it comes to learning material for test time.

Memory also works on certain laws:

First, is the law of recency. It's easier to remember things that happened recently than those that happened some time ago. For instance, let me ask you, what did you have for dinner last night? How about if I asked you, what did you have for dinner three weeks ago today?

Second, is the law of vividness. This means that we remember things that made the biggest impressions on us, were the most dramatic or extraordinary. For instance, you might remember what you did on your last holiday, but not what you did a month before when you stayed at home, unless of course, then too you did something striking, different, dramatic or extraordinary.

Third, the law of frequency says that we remember things we experience most often. This is why for instance you don't forget your name, your age, your address or the names of your friends.

For the student, the trick is to use recency, vividness and frequency when studying. Before a test or exam, recency will be important, having studied the material just before the test. Associating vividness through creating pictures or unusual acronyms will allow you to better remember the material under study. And using repetition, studying the material over and over again will create the frequency that maximizes your memory.

The Loci memory technique

A final technique is called loci. Loci was used by the ancient Greek orators to remember speeches. It combines using organization, visual memory and association. The first step is to imagine in your mind a common path that you walk. For instance, for me it is a walk from my house to a nearby pizza restaurant to buy dinner. What's important is that you have a clear picture of the path and the objects along it in your mind. Now take yourself on that familiar path, a path that you cover very often. I can see myself walking to the intersection and waiting for the walk light to signal my crossing. That's my first landmark.

Second when I cross the road I pass an ugly green house. Before I cross the road is a day care centre. Then as I cross the road, there is a mechanic's workshop. Finally the pizza shop. The number of landmarks chosen will depend on the number of things you want to remember. Each landmark could be an acronym to remember yet more sets of material or it could be a concept itself. To succeed in the ancient art of loci you need to create powerful visual associations for your material at each landmark.

Imagine for a moment I am attempting to remember the last 5 monarchs of England. At home, where I begin from, is Queen Elizabeth II, the current monarch. Leaving home through the bright sunroom, I am reminded of what Elizabeth has done to raise the character of the monarchy, perhaps only wondering slightly as I pass the rubbish bins at the gate, what her children have done to tarnish it.

As I reach the traffic lights, there is George VI. Like those traffic lights he maintained a sense of order in troublesome times, even remaining at Buckinghman Palace during the Nazi bombings of London in the second world war.

Then some metres past the traffic lights, is the ugly green house. I walk past quickly recalling the scant 11 month reign of Edward VIII who abdicated the throne after marrying an American divorcee. As I look at the green paintwork I recall the words much later of Edward's widow who lamented his abdication: "He might have been a great King; the people loved him." Indeed this house could have been beautiful if it wasn't such an ugly shade of green.

Next is the daycare centre. Here is George V, who married Mary of Teck who bore him 4 sons and 1 daughter.

Now as I cross the road I find myself at the mechanics workshop. There is a bright red sports car parked outside. Here is Edward VII, who something of a rebel during his younger life, died of a series of heart attacks in 1910.

Finally I am hungry now and it is a joy to reach the pizza shop, for here is Victoria, who enjoyed the longest, and some say fondest reign of any monarch in England. When she died an entire era died with her. Inside the pizza shop is a teenager waiting for a pizza with a walkman earpiece in his ear. I recall that even in Victoria's old age, she maintained a youthful energy and optimism that infected the population.

The system of loci can also be based around features in a room. This is particularly useful if you are giving a speech. With loci you can use parts of the room in which you are presenting the speech to represent associations with the material you need to remember in a clockwise fashion. Whatever loci landmarks you use, make the associations vivid and unforgettable.

Exercise 13

Now it is your turn to use the ancient orator's art of Loci to remember you own material for study success. In this exercise, let's take 8 key turning points during World War II:

1939	Sep 1	German army invades Poland
1939	Sep 3	Britain and France declare war on Germany
1940	May 10	Winston Churchill appointed British prime minister
1941	Dec 7	Japanese attack US navy base at Pearl Harbour
1944	Jun 6	D-Day: invasion of Europe begins - Allied landings at Normandy
1945	May 7	Unconditional surrender of all German forces
1945	Aug 6	First atomic bomb dropped – Hiroshima
1945	Aug 14	Unconditional surrender of Japanese forces

Now imagine a path that you are familiar with. See, hear and feel the 8 events of 1939 – 1945 to associate them with 8 landmarks along your path.

For each event listed describe the landmark alongside it, and how this landmark relates to the event and dates. Then close any notes and use the loci to test your recall.

Did you remember them all easily?

Exercise 14

In this next exercise, we're going to be looking at using loci in the same way that the ancient Greek orators did. When delivering a speech it is important to have a great start, and a great ending with organized and interesting material in the middle.

Imagine you have been asked to present a 3 minute speech on an interest or project.

Now select a room you know very well, and in which you could deliver this speech to a small audience.

For a 3 minute speech you will need 6 landmarks, 1 per 30 seconds. The first and last landmarks should be especially vivid so they get attention and leave your audience with something to think about.

Record the 6 main points and landmarks for your 3 minute speech. Now practice delivering the speech.

Principle 14: Know your learning style

Kevin was nervous as his mother opened his school report. She read down the list of grades... Mathematics 97% and smiled... but that smile quickly turned to a frown as she came to English, 43%...

Why is it that some students achieve top results in one subject yet really struggle in other subjects? Perhaps you find that you're better with language subjects such as English or history rather than logical subjects such as Mathematics and Physics? I'm sure you know others who are brilliant in language or logical subjects but not in both. Yet, the mark of a successful student is that he or she can achieve excellence in all subject areas.

In most cases students who are brilliant in logical subjects but only average or below in language subjects have failed to grasp the techniques needed to use their mind in expressive ways rather than in logical processes. It is the same the other way around. In *Part IV* we're going to be looking at specific principles for mastering language and mathematics oriented subjects. Meanwhile, I need to share with you some very important research into why some students find some subjects easier than others. More importantly you're going to become aware of the way you learn, and how, to reach total study success you can counter your innate learning style by adapting it to subjects in which your comfort zone is weaker.

In his ground breaking book, *Frames of Mind: The Theory of Multiple Intelligences*, Howard Gardener, a neuropsychologist from Harvard University proposes seven different human competencies. Students will find they possess certain competencies in lesser or greater degrees. The possession of certain competencies leads to distinctive ways of thinking and approaching problems.

It is important to remember that different subjects and settings will require different approaches. The lesson here is that where you do not naturally operate with the competency required for a certain subject, you will need to invest more time in learning the approaches required for that subject.

The first competency or "intelligence" as it is called, is linguistic intelligence. Simply this relates to your intelligence in reading and writing. Linguistically intelligent individuals are likely to excel in English, history and other subjects that involve the use of language. Linguistically intelligent individuals thrive and are drawn to careers such as those in journalism, writing or teaching.

The second competency is logical mathematical intelligence. This relates to your ability with numbers, mathematics and problem solving. Students that possess this intelligence are naturally drawn to mathematical and logical subjects including sciences. They are drawn toward careers in computer programming, engineering or mathematics.

The third competency is visual-spatial intelligence. Students possessing this intelligence are particularly good with visual media. They excel in subjects and career fields which use their creativity such as in art and design. Visual-spatial people have a sense of beauty and perspective.

The fourth competency is body-kinesthetic intelligence. This relates to how well an individual is able to operate at a physical level. Body-kinesthetic intelligence is most relevant in sports, athletics, dancing and the use of tools or handiwork.

The fifth competency is musical rhythmic intelligence. This refers to abilities with music and rhythm. Students with high musical rhythmic intelligence find learning and succeeding with a musical instrument easier than other students.

The sixth competency is interpersonal intelligence. This refers to an individual's ability to communicate and get along with others. If you have high interpersonal intelligence you are likely to be a good communicator, enjoy talking to others, and you have the ability to work well in groups and teams, possibly in leadership roles. People with high interpersonal intelligences succeed in people oriented professions such as sales, marketing and politics.

Finally there is intrapersonal intelligence. This refers to how well you can manage yourself and work alone. People with high levels of intrapersonal intelligence are very good in self management and working independently.

These seven intelligences represent a powerful contribution to the body of research on teaching and learning. For study success, students need to consider their levels of intelligence in each area. For example a student who has high linguistic intelligence but low logical mathematical intelligence needs to consider that their learning style is more linguistic than mathematical.

Now that student, currently not doing so well in mathematics, through active study can learn mathematics from a linguistic perspective. What do I mean by this? If you are linguistically intelligent but mathematically a dunce, don't try to learn mathematics from a purely mathematical point of view. You need to approach mathematics from a linguistic point of view where your numerical understanding is assisted by language.

What I've noticed, and indeed has been my own case, is that many top English students succeed in mathematics by considering the solution of a certain type of problem as a series of steps that can be explained and identified by language. On the other hand students who are strong in mathematics are able to succeed in English by considering tasks such as a literary essay as a logical process involving a formula of showing, explaining and proving.

The study of multiple intelligences is also important when considering your likely career direction. Many careers require multiple intelligences. For example an architect will require some linguistic intelligence to write design briefs, some mathematical intelligence to perform essential calculations, a great deal of visual-spatial intelligence to achieve creative building designs and certain amounts of interpersonal and intrapersonal intelligence to manage clients and themselves. A doctor would require linguistic, logical, intrapersonal and very strong interpersonal skills.

It's now time to consider your competencies and intelligences. This analysis will help you to consider how to learn in each subject. It will help make you aware of your weaknesses and strengths and how to approach your studies for the best results. Remember, just because you operate at a lower level in one or more of the intelligences, does not mean you can't succeed in a subject requiring that intelligence. All intelligences are built with practice and study.

Exercise 15

Rank your competency in each intelligence on a scale of 1-10, 1 being your weakest, and 10 being your strongest:

Linguistic intelligence – ability to use language well.

Logical mathematical intelligence – ability to do well in mathematics and logic.

Visual spatial intelligence – ability in artistic areas such as painting or sculpture.

Body kinesthetic intelligence – ability to do well in sports or physical activities.

Musical rhythmic intelligence – ability to do well in music.

Interpersonal intelligence – ability to work and learn well in groups and get along with other people.

Intrapersonal intelligence – ability to learn and work well alone.

Interpreting the results:

Consider your two highest rankings as an indication of your strongest "intelligence grouping":

1. If it includes linguistic intelligence, understand that you are strong in writing, reading and language. You probably learn things best when they are expressed in language. In learning you will understand most quickly through language explanations.

2. If it includes logical mathematical intelligence, understand that you learn best through approaches that use logical, mathematical or formulaic processes. In learning you will learn most quickly by logical, numerical or step by step explanations.

3. If it includes visual spatial intelligence, understand that you are strong in visualizing and working with physical structures or shapes. You probably learn best through seeing patterns or the physical aspects of what you're learning. Attempt to visualize and picture what you are trying to learn.

4. If it includes body kinesthetic intelligence, understand that experiencing what you're trying to learn physically is an important part of your learning style. When learning new things attempt to find ways to engage your body and sense of feeling in the subject studied.

5. If it includes musical rhythmic intelligence, understand that you respond well to music and rhythm and you may be able to experience accelerated learning by engaging music and rhythm in study and memorization.

6. If it includes interpersonal intelligence, understand that you will probably learn best when you work with a group or team. This may involve studying with likeminded friends or ideally working closely with a good tutor in your study programme.

7. If it includes intrapersonal intelligence, this is advantageous considering the concentration successful study requires. It will mean you have a fairly good chance of disciplining yourself and achieving the solitary concentration often required for study success.

Ideally the two best intelligences to appear in the highest rank for academic study success are "intrapersonal intelligence" with either "linguistic" or "logical mathematical" intelligence. However it must be remembered that in life the other intelligences can be equally as important. Interpersonal intelligence is extremely important in the modern corporate world as employers want to employ good communicators who work well in teams. Creativity is vital to the success of many careers and especially artistic or entrepreneurial efforts. Yet creativity may depend on strong "visual spatial", "body kinesthetic" or "musical rhythmic" intelligences.

What is most important to remember is that even now, if you may perceive yourself weak in some of the intelligences, they are as much developable skills as they are innate intelligences or "born talents". With patient concentration and dedicated effort you can gain strong intelligences in any of the seven areas, just as a pro-golfer perfects his game with hours of practice on the course.

Genius is 99 percent perspiration and 1 percent inspiration.

- Albert Einstein

You have now begun an important journey into preparing yourself for lifelong learning. You are now a student who can approach any subject and reach excellence in it. In this part we focused on accelerating your learning and improving your memory. You learned the principles of leaping all obstacles, showing off your skills, accessing a river of flow, harnessing the magic of memory and knowing your learning style.

The first 14 principles are your foundation. Go back over them in your mind, using the method of loci.

Principle 1:   Stretch your mind
Principle 2:   Solve problems & answer questions
Principle 3:   Find driving forces/motivational bases
Principle 4:   Do each part well
Principle 5:   Relate it to life
Principle 6:   Learn from failure
Principle 7:   Focus for results
Principle 8:   Make a plan for the future
Principle 9:   Gain total self confidence in studies
Principle 10: Leap the obstacles
Principle 11: Show off your skill
Principle 12: Access a river of flow
Principle 13: Harness the magic of memory
Principle 14: Know your learning style

In part IV we'll be looking at the remaining 3 highly specific principles of mastering English, mastering Mathematics, and mastering tests, exams, essays and assignments. Thank you for journeying with me up until now.

Part IV: Specific tools for success

Principle 15: Master English, reading & writing

Having mastered the principles of how to study, it is now that we come to mastery in specific subjects. Core subjects to any study are English and Mathematics. If you understand the techniques to succeed in English you'll be well equipped to succeed in other linguistic subjects such as history, geography and economics. Similarly If you understand the techniques to succeed in Mathematics you will be well equipped to succeed in other mathematical or logical subjects such as science, physics, chemistry and computer programming.

First we come to principle 15, master English, reading and writing to ensure you have the linguistic ability to succeed not only in English, but all subjects requiring language which is basically *all* subjects. English as a subject, is something like an egg. It has two parts and when you crack the shell there is so much you can do with it.

English language – "the egg-yolk"

The first part of English is the yolk. This is the core structure of the language. English is made up of vocabulary or words. Words only exist because we give them meaning. Human beings are unique in that they appear specifically designed to learn and process complex languages. Being able to speak, listen, read and write words is one of the many awesome and fascinating features that make us human. Language can be so complex, intricate and beautiful, it is one of the great wonders of human life that it can be learned so readily by babies.

The key to enhancing your language ability throughout life is exposure. Top students constantly expose themselves to language through reading. But consider for a moment just how important exposure to language really is, especially while growing up. Imagine the true story of Kamala and Amala. In 1920 some Indian villagers discovered a wolf mother in her den together with four cubs. Two were baby wolves, but the other two were human children. These two children were later named Kamala and Amala. Kamala was about eight years old and Amala was one and a half. The sisters acted and behaved much like wolves. They were used to going on all fours. Their teeth had a sharp edge, they moved their nostrils sniffing for food and they ate raw meat. At night they prowled like wolves. Sometimes they howled. The diary of Reverend Singh remains today. He took charge of the two girls, placing them in his orphanage. In 1921 he wrote: "The other children tried their utmost to allure them to play with them, but this they resented very much, and would frighten them by opening their jaws, showing their teeth, and at times making for them with a peculiar harsh noise."

Amala only lived one year in human habitation, but Kamala survived until the age of eighteen. She learned to speak a few words but her vocabulary was only thought to consist of about 30 words, many of them not common to English speech.

On the other hand there is the happier case of Isabelle. Unlike Kamala and Amala who were removed from all human society, from when Isabelle was a baby she had been given only enough attention to sustain her life. Nobody spoke to her. Her mother was deaf and could not speak. It wasn't until Isabelle was six that she was discovered. She had no language and her mental development was lower than an average two-year old, even at the age of six. Yet after being discovered she took her place at an ordinary school and after only a year spoke about as well as the other students in her class.

These two cases demonstrate the importance of exposure to language and that there is probably an important stage of human development, or a critical period in which language learning takes place. This may also be seen with students who come to English from a second language. Although adults will attempt to speak the new language, many young children appear confused and horrified to hear speech they cannot understand. They may stop talking for weeks or even months. Yet in the long run, the result is completely the opposite, for the children soon sound just like native speakers, whereas the adults never lose the accent from their first language or their hesitation in the new language.

These findings point to strong evidence that there is a sensitive period in learning the yolk or structure of language. However, in the subject of English all students are seeking to polish their written and spoken English. The yolk component of English is made up of words and sentence structures.

To succeed in English you need a good knowledge of the yolk, of grammar and how to put it together and shape writing.

The outside aspect of English that proceeds when you know how to use the language is the study of literature. The study of stories, novels, plays and poems. This side of English looks at how language is used to create believable stories and to express feelings and ideas.

First, lets have a look at improving the core part of English, the yolk, the writing and construction part of the language and subject.

Top students in English know how to use words and string them together. This is important in all essay and examination work for English. Writing is a lot like dressing for a party. You have to match things together to achieve a good look.

In English the first rule is to make sure the writing meets the purpose it was written for. In an essay you'll be answering a question. If you were writing an email to your friend your intention would be entirely different. Perhaps giving your friend something to laugh about for example. Too many students have one single writing style that they think can be used to cover all tasks. But to be a great writer is much like being a great actor. You have to be able to fill many different roles. That's why for instance Harrison Ford plays a roguish smuggler pilot in *Star Wars*, yet an intelligent and sophisticated Doctor in *The Fugitive*. Your writing should also be great acting. In an essay on *The Catcher in the Rye* for instance, it might be sharp, exact and reflective to achieve an inspiring answer. On the other hand in a creative thriller story the writing may twist to give a feeling that is entirely different.

"But I have my own style of writing. I can't change that," you protest.

Try to imagine building such a degree of writing skill that you can flex it and change it according to the purpose that's required.

The second rule is to be very clear and very precise. Do not leave points that are cloudy, ambiguous or do not answer the question in essays or exams. Good writing is clear writing. The reader does not become frustrated, doubtful, uncertain or bored. The reader is carried into a rich harvest of ideas that impress him or her with vivid colours of meaning.

"But how do I make my writing clearer and more flexible?" you might ask. The first step is to look at the words you use themselves. Your knowledge and skill with words is directly related to how much you read. But more about that later. For now the main staple words you will find yourself using to construct phrases in which to express yourself are verbs (doing words), nouns (naming words) and adjectives (describing words).

That's what brings us to our third rule. Use better words: Better verbs, nouns, adjectives and adverbs. Let me give you some examples. An ordinary writer might construct a sentence that reads:

"The man walked into the office and stole the money."

Notice the verb in the sentence is "walked".
A skilled writer might construct that same sentence reading:

"The man tiptoed into the office and swiped the money."

The word tiptoed is much more vivid and informative than the plainer word walked. The word swiped is faster and more aggressive than stole. Tiptoed tells us how the man walked. Swiped tells us how the man stole.
In the same way we can make our nouns much more powerful.
Let's say we now have the new improved version of our sentence, which is:

"The man tiptoed into the office and swiped the money."

A skilled writer could add interest and information to the nouns to give a more vivid meaning and idea of this story that the sentence tells.
For instance, instead of:

"The man tiptoed into the office and swiped the money."

He or she may have:

"The thief tiptoed into the office and swiped the cashbox."

Notice how the nouns give more information and colour to the sentence.

Starting to use more descriptive verbs and nouns is extremely important when we consider using better adjectives and adverbs. Particularly in creative writing many students like to overuse adjectives and adverbs. Your reader should be able to form their own descriptions of the scene or issue without you having to describe it with an overdose of adjectives and adverbs. These describing words are often clumsy when overused because everyone has their own interpretation of adjectives and adverbs. Take the adjective "happy" and the adverb "happily" for instance. To one reader happy just means not being miserable. To another reader happy could mean a state of complete bliss. Instead descriptive nouns, verbs and strong settings and structures give a far clearer sense of meaning to all readers.

Exercise 16

Rewrite the following sentences improving the use of verbs, nouns, adjectives and adverbs to make them more descriptive (use your imagination to adjust the tone and style).

Note:

Verbs - give the action of the sentence. Better verbs give a clearer sense of mood or degree of action.

Nouns - name things and can also give description by the choice of name.

Adjectives - describe a noun, adverbs - describe a verb.

Example:

BEFORE: Jack fell down the big rocky hill uncontrollably
AFTER: Jack tumbled down the mountain

Sentences to rewrite:

1. Humpty had a really disastrous fall from the large brick fence.

2. Georgie who had a large, round and fat stomach, kissed Veronica quickly and suddenly on her pretty cheek.

3. Pat barely managed to live in the large substantial shoe where she fed, clothed and taught many scruffy and underfed children.

4. Goldilocks was a young female house robber who carefully sought out happy and comfortable families of bears.

5. Cinderella stepped upwards into the vehicle, one bare foot strangely yet meaningfully missing a shoe.

6. The kind and handsome man was poorly informed as he walked up to the sleeping beauty.

7. The Queen looked quickly into the mirror at first, but then she looked fixedly and angrily after seeing the girl.

8. Snow White was a tall, slender and very beautiful woman who supposedly engaged the differing personality types of many much shorter but conscientious old men.

9. Sleeping Beauty lay silently and completely asleep, her stomach round and large and bulgingly pregnant since Prince Charming knew so much of the big wide world yet so little of the delicate art of kissing.

Figurative Language

You now understand that good writing is a lot about selecting the right words. Beyond using better nouns and verbs, streamlining the use of adjectives and adverbs is most effectively done by using figurative language. Figurative language is basically language that draws on some other association, usually visual, to give a layer of extra meaning. Simply speaking it is the figurative language that so often makes writing exciting. However the trick with figurative language is not to overuse it. If the reader senses you're trying to use figurative techniques just for the sake of them, you'll lose all credibility. We're going to be having a look now at the secrets of great writing through using figurative devices.

First, let's take a look at visual devices. These include metaphors, similes, analogies and personification. Metaphors are the most powerful of these devices and they can exist once or throughout an entire essay or story. For example, imagine you are analyzing a story in which the main character, Jacob tricks a number of his friends. You may choose to use a snooker metaphor, particularly if it is a game that Jacob plays throughout the story:

"Jacob was a snooker player, and Mary was the final 8-ball waiting to be removed from the table of his life."

Metaphors are direct. Jacob was the snooker player. Mary was the 8-ball.

On the other hand similes are less direct, they typically use the words like or as to distance the expression:

For example, "Jacob was like a snooker player when it come to running his life…"

"The dead body was as cold and fresh as a washed up fish."

Analogies are stories used to make or emphasize a point. They need to be very closely related to the point, clever or memorable to work effectively. Often they are well used in speeches. For example, a sports coach was once delivering a speech about his job. He began with the analogy of a ship coming into harbour:

"The captain of the ship become angry for there was the light from a fishing boat blocking his path. 'Move at once' he bellowed over the radio, 'this is the captain of the ship, we're coming into harbour.' There was no reply. 'For the second time, move it', the captain hollered down the radio. Finally as he was about to threaten the little fishing boat with a coming collision, there was a reply. 'This is the lighthouse, back up, you're approaching rocks.'"

Our speaker went on to discuss how his role as a coach, was often like that of a lighthouse. He then used the imagery of the boats and the sea as similes and metaphors throughout the rest of his speech to great effect.

Another career woman was asked to write an exciting news piece on her job as a marketing executive. She begun with a real world analogy:

"It is 7am and I'm screaming. That's because I'm sitting in a small black tire hurtling down the black water rapids of a cave that seems at least fifty feet underground. I don't know what's going to be around the next bend, and but for the light on my helmet I would see nothing. All I can hear around me is the screams of my fellow tire riders...

Well, that was a trip I took a year ago on a black water rafting adventure. It's a lot like my job. Exciting, action packed and so often filled with the fear of not knowing what's around the next corner."

Finally personification is a form of metaphor that involves giving something non-human, human characteristics. This helps your reader, presumably a human, relate to the action. The trees chattered in the wind, the waves danced across the sand and the cars ate up the rally track are all examples of personification.

Beyond visual and association devices, sound devices can add interest and spice to writing. Onomatopoeia involves using words that sound like their action, such as bang, crash, zoom and whiz. Alliteration involves repeating the opening sounds of words to make them memorable, such as the "slip, slop, slap" sun burn commercial. That's for slip on a t-shirt, slop on a hat and slap on suntan lotion to be safe in the sun. This commercial also used a degree of onomatopoeia creating a jingle people would remember in sunny weather.

There are also style devices such as rhetorical question, imperatives, quotations, irony, parody and pun. Rhetorical questions are asked primarily in speeches. They are questions raised to the audience or reader with the aim of making them think, since they are physically unable to answer your question directly to you.

For example imagine you were asked to write an essay exploring friendship. A beginning with a captivating question would serve to draw in the reader, for example:

"Could you imagine a life where you're completely alone? Where you have no friends or nobody to talk to on a daily basis? How would this affect you and who you are?"

Imperatives involve the use of direct commands. They give a sense of urgency and action to writing. For example, at the end that essay exploring friendship the writer may order us: "Treasure your friends, do not neglect or forget them. Be there for them and they will be there for you!"

In essay work and indeed most non-fiction writing, quotations are very powerful, especially from famous or trusted sources. An essay on the topic of the Government for instance would benefit from quoting a source such as John F Kennedy, who once said:

"Ask not what your country can do for you, but what can you do for your country."

Notice too in that line, the balance of the sentence. At the "but" the sentence is a seesaw of meaning creating a memorable structure.

Irony, parody and pun are forms of humour that can be added to writing to give spice and vitality. Irony is where the meaning is actually the opposite of what is intended. For example:

"That's such a beautiful dress you're wearing… did it belong to your grandmother?"

Or "Did you hear about the burglar who had his getaway car stolen from outside the house he was robbing?"

On the other hand, parody is just as much fun, for it makes fun of other literary works, styles or even characters and people themselves. For example…

"Romeo, Romeo, where art thou pre-nuptial agreement…"

Or "Nike, just pay it…"

Puns make use of a double meaning for their sense of fun and usually rely on homonyms or expressions with dual meanings. For example:

"When the fashion magazine asked the model how much to do a cover shoot at the football stadium, she gave them a ball park figure."

"Jonathan, stop looking daggers at your boss."
"Why?"
"Because he might give you the chop."

"Doctor, I've got a steering wheel stuck between my legs… It's driving me nuts."

Additionally poetic justice is often used in stories. As with irony it can be a very satisfying element for readers. Poetic justice is where someone receives an unforeseen but well-deserved reward or retribution. A fascinating example of this is the fate of Richard Bentley, the publisher who diddled Charles Dickens in his early career. Dickens got his own back by naming the wife-beating sadist in *Great Expectations* Bentley Drummle. It is more than likely that as the work became successful and widely known, everyone in literary London got the point.

The style of the writing, particularly in story telling will also have much to do with the narrative voice and point of view. The narrative voice refers to how the story is told and by whom. Most stories are told in either the first person or the third person and mostly from the point of view of the main character. It is best to write in a narrative voice that comes naturally to you and to use the point of view to help the reader understand and relate better to a character or to the style and mood of the story.

Finally, good writing entertains and informs the reader in a way so absorbing they forget the effort of reading and become entangled in the message or story. To achieve good writing you need to use the best nouns, verbs and descriptive words. You need to use carefully selected language techniques that add to the visual colour of your message. And humour always goes a long way to add a smile in communication. This needs to be put together in paragraphs. Remember one paragraph, one idea. You then need to consider your tense and tone. Maintain the same tense throughout your writing passage, whether that be past, present or future tense. And watch the tone – if it's a formal essay, stick to a formal tone. If it's an informal story you can make it more chatty and conversational.

Exercise 17

Imagine for a moment a beach with a beautiful sunset above the ocean. It appears deserted, that is except for two people walking where the waves nip the sand, hand in hand. Visualize this picture, and for each of the examples below, form your own descriptions using the appropriate language technique:

Metaphor:
"The sun is an angel warming us with her rays, despite the cold water."

Simile:
"Our conversation flows like ice cream, sweet and perfect on a hot day."

Personification:
"The rocks bite at our feet and nibble at our ankles."

Onomatopoeia:
"The waves no longer crash on to the beach and now swish the sand calmly."

Imperative:
"Walk with me on the beach my friend so that we may remember the old times."

Irony:
"If you don't like someone's company walk a lonely beach with them."

Pun
"There were waves of joy as the tide turned against that big fish who was my boss."

English Literature – "the egg-white"

The yolk, or language side of the subject of English consists of the tools and techniques we've just been discussing. The other side to the subject of English is the literature or the egg-white. It is in literature that language is used at its finest, and through literature that the stories of culture and learning shine through. Through understanding literature we increase our understanding of the world. What happens when we read or listen is that we are exposed to the thoughts and research of others. We are forced to actively consider and think about a much bigger world than the one we immediately inhabit. The power of literature takes us from one reality to another. Through literature we can experience the lives of kings, murderers, millionaires and the homeless.

Top students instinctively have a love for literature and a desire to read. In fact it is so often reading that distinguishes the top students from the poor to average. Let me give you an example of two brothers, both of them immigrants. The brothers were very close in age, with only a year between them. The elder brother, we'll call him William, had little interest in reading. He was a television man. No matter how much he was encouraged to read more, he would not read more than 1 book every 2 or 3 months. On the other hand, his younger brother, we'll call him David, read voraciously. David was addicted to reading. He ploughed through books like some kind of psychotic librarian. He read, on average, 1-2 books per week and he covered a wide area from popular fiction such as Stephen King, to classical literature such as Dickens and Poe through to non-fiction books in subjects he was interested in such as future trends and the sport of the Frisbee.

Some years later William and David went on to tertiary studies and in time moved out into the world of work. At this stage the difference in language skill between William and David was very pronounced in both senses. As you might expect David's ability in speech and writing was ahead of William's. This meant that David found it easier to find high paying work as a young adult compared to his brother.

These two brothers didn't begin from startlingly different levels. In fact William had many advantages over David due to the fact that he had a more outgoing nature. Yet, the experience demonstrated powerfully the lasting enriching benefits of an active reading diet.

Read all you can. Reading is a lot like skiing. At first the results are not instant, and it takes time before you enjoy it. Just as you have to get to the ski slope, don ski clothes and learn to keep yourself upright, so you have to find a good book, get into it and begin to enjoy the ride. Once inside a book that genuinely interests you, you have opened the doors to a new exciting world inside your mind.

But how do you find books that genuinely interest you? Learn to explore your library. Get to know the non-fiction areas you like and what types of themes you like in fiction books. I often issue three times as many books as I need, because I know that only one in three books will interest and engage me, even after selection. If I begin a book and become frustrated or bored with it, I return it to the library hoping that it will not inflict the same misery it did on me to others. Meanwhile I plough into books that do grab my attention and keep me reading. As you read more and more, your reading speed becomes faster, and your reading appetite becomes greater. Your awareness increases and your confidence goes up.

In the subject of English literature you'll be close reading texts and inevitably answering questions on them, usually in the form of essay questions. In English essays you need to remember the acronym of S.E.E… for Show, Explain and provide an Example.

For instance lets assume for a moment an essay topic asks you to discuss the relationship that forms between Romeo and Juliet in that play by William Shakespeare…

Let me show you an argument that makes use of S.E.E… Showing, explaining and giving an example:

Example of a S.E.E. discussion on the relationship between Romeo and Juliet:

Shakespeare's first tragedy deals with ardent young love against a backdrop of family feuding, hatred and at last death. The Italian setting gives rise to a passionate environment of street quarreling, ardent lovers and romantic moonlit nights. Romeo is an emotional character and very prone to strong feeling. He is still recovering from an unsatisfied infatuation with the beautiful Rosalind. His capacity for a new girlfriend seems to be intensified.

Meanwhile there is mention of Juliet's future marriage plans. She is at a time of transition in her life. Like Romeo, she is also a ripe character. As in many great romances, Romeo and Juliet meet and fall in love with the poignancy of coincidence and through the hand of fate. Their youth, ardor and instant chemistry sets off a chain reaction between them.

Romeo's infatuation, and his contribution to the relationship is that of the gallant and brave young lover, masculine, enthusiastic and physical. In a dreamy moment he looks on Juliet and says

"See, how she leans her cheek upon her hand!
O, that I were a glove upon that hand,
That I might touch that cheek!"

For Juliet, a girl of fourteen love is something previously unknown. It is both frightening and blissful at the same time. Yet she develops through trial and sorrow to that of a heroic woman passionately in love. She says:

"Give me my Romeo; and when he shall die,
Take him and cut him out in little stars,
And he will make the face of heaven so fine
That all the world will be in love with night
And pay no worship to the garish sun."

The relationship of Romeo and Juliet demonstrates the power of human love in the face of adversity. It demonstrates the magnetism of first love and the welding of realised infatuation, until the love itself becomes a force greater than the characters own selves.

This analysis on the nature of the relationship in Romeo & Juliet could well fill an essay of 3,000 words or more, yet the important point is to notice how points were proven with the very lines from the play as spoken by Romeo and Juliet. The lesson here is to make strong, clear and precise arguments backed up with evidence, usually in the form of quotes taken directly from the literature under study.

In answering literary questions you must be clear and precise. You must answer the question exactly. And you must show, explain and give an example for each of your arguments. Beyond an introduction that sets up your approach, each point of the argument ought to form one paragraph until the conclusion is reached, in which the final findings and answer is confirmed.

Literature questions are often directed at setting, character, plot, theme or the language style and structure used to achieve the mood and feeling of all of these. The setting is the area or location in which the story exists, and you ought to look out for the style, mood or constraints of the environment described. The characters people the story and it is often their strength, realism and ability to engage some kind of relationship with the reader that makes the story great. The plot is what happens in the story, and will most often consist of a "lead-in" that sets the action, a "climax point" at which excitement or interest peaks and then a "denouement" which sees the unraveling and finalizing of the story.

Themes are the underlying ideas that shape the literature. They are the aspects of life that the literature addresses. A powerful theme of Romeo and Juliet is young love. The language style of Romeo and Juliet has both poetic and tragic qualities, sometimes like a lover's letter, sometimes like a funeral's eulogy. The play along with many others by Shakespeare is written in the iambic pentameter rhyme scheme. A rhyme scheme that has a distinctive *da-dum da-dum da-dum rhythm.* When read aloud such verse naturally follows a beat, alike to that of a human heart beat at rest.

Finally it is useful to consider how stories are written and how an author's own life and personality impacts on this. The international publishing business today, at least for works of fiction, functions through literary agents. Since the chances of having an unsolicited manuscript published in the US or UK are extremely rare, writers must first find a good literary agent to represent them. Literary agents only take on the best manuscripts and most promising clients, often specializing in particular genres of fiction. Through this system the agents act to create a screening process for publishers, who then consider submissions from reputable agents. In the business of writing books, the relationship between the author and the literary agent is a vital one. Typically literary agents are available to discuss ideas and suggest improvements to manuscripts before they are submitted.

That's why in exploring the best principles of fiction writing, the best place to look is in the findings of successful literary agents. As a student of language and writing it is worthwhile considering these principles in your own reading and writing.

Harris, Harris & Donahue represent authors from the UK, US, Canada and elsewhere. On their web site they ask writers to consider a checklist for good writing before they submit their manuscript. Some of the basic important points for consideration are as follows:

1. The writing should prove the premise or the reason for the story.
2. The reader should be touched emotionally through the writing.
3. The characters should appear real and believable.
4. The characters should change, grow, discover and develop throughout the story.
5. The characters should be involved in escalating conflicts.
6. The conflicts within the story should be resolved by the end.
7. There should be variety in the writing.
8. The events of the story should grow out of each other.
9. The climax should have impact, and be satisfying.
10. Irony and poetic justice can be very satisfying for the reader.
11. Extraneous or unneeded bits of business should be cut out to keep the writing tight.
12. It is important to choose the best narrative voice and point of view.
13. All possible conflicts in the story should be exploited for dramatic effect.
14. Symbols can be a powerful tool when appropriate and significant to the story.
15. Each scene should have a rising conflict and move the story forward.
16. Every line of dialogue (conversation) should develop either characters or the story.
17. The writing should be sensual, appealing to all five senses. The reader should be able to taste, feel, see, hear and smell what the characters do.
18. The writing should be more active than passive, and characters should actually do things.
19. Action should take place in the story, not just be reported as having happened in the past or in another place.
20. Good writers show, not tell, so that readers feel they saw the events themselves.

In summing up to master the subject of English, build your writing skill by using better nouns and verbs and by using adjectives and adverbs judiciously. Actively practice using figurative language techniques that give richness and colour to your writing without overdoing it. Learn the art of sprinkling a garnish of irony or parody to add humour to your work. Read to expand your mind, your knowledge and your understanding of language usage and the world at large. Learn how to approach literature analysis using the S.E.E. formula and understanding the workings of setting, characters, plots and themes in the construction of a story. And, last of all, the three most important things to better master language and English: reading, reading and more reading.

Exercise 18

This exercise looks at the first chapter of a novel, "Tokyo Curry" (extract follows). The question to answer is:

Discuss how the language style and techniques used establish the mood of this chapter.

Use the following format to write your answer:

1. Introduction – set up purpose and objective of discussion (1 paragraph)

2. Body – paragraphed points making clear arguments according to S.E.E. formula (3-4 paragraphs)

3. Conclusion – outline findings and final answer (1 paragraph)

The text for analysis and discussion:

TOKYO CURRY
An extract from the novel

Chapter One

It was a body for sure, cold, fresh and dead.
'Just like a big dead fish washed up,' was Yamakawa's first thought.
The fat man had dented his way across the sand to investigate. Now he wished he hadn't. None of this was his business. His red rubbery face was contorted, looking like one big smacked backside. Kenzin, his dog, an Akita of dubious breed was sniffing at the head.

'You've got no respect, have you dog?'

Yamakawa hated corpses, even though he was no stranger to them. They always left a bitter taste in his mouth requiring half a gallon of Sake to fix. This particular one, its shape, its weight, reminded him of a cadaver he'd loaded into an old Toyota Crown at the back of a Yokohama warehouse. But this wasn't those days, far from them. And this wasn't the typical sort of corpse that washes up in a cold winter's night in Tokyo Bay.

The fleshy man sniffed at the corpse.

'The trouble with this city,' he considered, 'is that the air always smells like it's had the life burnt out of it anyway.' That was true. The chilly breeze carried smog that oozed from traffic, factories and the breathing of twelve million people. As Yamakawa knew, but had never become used to in fifty odd years, not only did the air smell, it was noisy. The night was a mortician's sponge soaking up the hubbub of the night market, bugle horns of ships, moaning traffic from Rainbow Bridge, banshee shrieks of emergency sirens and the huffing, puffing uneasy nights of the living.

If the night sounds and smells of this city could be defined in one headline, one single title in Yamakawa's old dark mind, it would've been "Hell's Orchestra in a Refrigerator."

And there was conductor Yamakawa! Good at describing, at labeling, at putting complex rot into words. He wasn't a smart man though. Not unless you reasoned that his smartest qualities lay in the fact that he always presented himself as a simple man. A dummy. In that was the greatest ambush.

Like corpses, he knew a bit about ambushes. He'd controlled half the Pachinko Parlors over four blocks once. That was no mean feat for the son of a *salaryman*. Now, right here in his retirement, walking Kenzin the lazy Akita, he found corpses. Most of his generation were packaging themselves off on tour buses in New Zealand and snapping everything on film from massive trees to grandkids cuddling sheep. Not him. Trouble crossed his palms like jam on a donut. Speaking of donuts, he was carrying a few too many of them, thanks to *Dunkim Donuts*, which he enjoyed more than his wife's company.

'You're a sick puppy Yamakawa san,' he said to Kenzin, but more to himself. You see he was just going to walk away.

'A corpse? So what! A *Gaijin*, dead, washed up in Tokyo Bay? How is it my fault if he mixed with the wrong crowd in Roppongi? Too bad, he was going to the bar. He'd chat up that Yuko for a bit… You may be old Yamakawa San, but you ain't lost your charm boy!'

Kenzin whined, sounding like a violin at the end of a tragic show. Yamakawa looked like the kind of man that would have kicked the dog. But he couldn't. He wouldn't. Didn't have a single violent bone in his body, all things considered. Now that was some kind of anger management given his years of experience on the fringes of the *Yakuza*. And he was too old for that game now, too old to yodel for his yen anymore. He could've run for political office, been a great dad. It was too late now. He took a donut from his bag and began munching.

The flesh of the corpse looked soft, purplish and pale. Just like his donut, typical *Gaijin*, undercooked. The cold sea had preserved the body. Yet a dark spider of veins running from the mouth to the gaping eyeballs indicated death had arrived with some agony.

'Yamakawa, you're a born coward, walk away man,' he told himself. But those blue eyes were genuine, even if they were dead. They were pleading with him, playing with his mind, damn it! This kid had a thick crop of blond hair, heavy and wet and strong from youth. He was an all American boy, no doubt about that. He might have been twenty-two. Yamakawa checked himself. You could never tell with *Gaijin* though, they always looked older than they really were. They had it easy too. He could see this kid, walking under elm trees, pretty girl on his arm, in college, all set for a life with two cars in the garage and a big lawn to cut.

'The problem with getting old,' it suddenly occurred to Yamakawa, was that you got soft. That was it, a big radish going soft right at the point of decay.

Now in earlier, more ambitious days you might say, he would have checked the pockets for a wallet and taken whatever yen notes were there, adding them to the fat roll in his own jacket pocket.

'Sick puppy,' he reminded himself. Kenzin looked at him in agreement.

Strangely he didn't examine the pockets in the saturated jeans for a wallet. He pulled out his little Nokia.

'Yeah, so much for loyalty to Japanese product,' he mused.

The fat arthritic thumb struggled to flip through the address book, revealing his stub from a missing fifth finger.

'Bingo!' it was the twentieth number, Ishigawa San. The middle-aged cop would be surprised to hear from him, no doubt. He would come down in ten, armed with his Nambu-made .38 caliber, and the little honey, policewoman Kato, his partner and intern by his side. She had the looks but not the gun though. That served as a reminder that in Japan men still had the upper hand. Right down to the police force, the man had the gun, the woman had the whistle. Shame this *Gaijin* kid wasn't gonna see that.

'Ishigawa San. I've found something, well someone, you may be interested in.'

He could hear the cogs in the old detective's brain grinding over. What favor was Yamakawa trying to bargain for now?

'What is it?' Ishigawa asked in that same earnest voice he'd had from those early days as a young constable in Roppongi.

'A *Gaijin*, probably American: Early twenties, blond hair, six foot perhaps, washed up in the bay, right below the fish market.'

'What does this have to do with you? I'd thought you'd retired?' asked the earnest voice on the end of the line.

Ishigawa's voice sounded small. Mind you, it was a tiny little thing this phone, could well have got lost in his ear, Yamakawa considered.

'I am retired but an old man's gotta get some exercise.' He would tease his old sparring partner for a bit. 'You know, take the dog for a walk now and again.'

'If any of these foreigners have anything to do with you old boy, the devil himself won't stop me taking you off the streets!' came the curt voice out of the little phone.

'Ooo, I'm scared... Wow, career cop eh?' Yamakawa hissed sarcastically, but then quickly added, 'Look I'm a good boy now, regular born again Buddha if you must know. I was simply having a stroll on the beach and he washed up in front of me. I'm just helping you do your job. Want to give something back to the community and all that. Now look...' Yamakawa proceeded to give him the exact location. Twenty minutes later officer Ishigawa and junior officer Kato of the Tokyo Metropolitan Police arrived at the beach to see a dead *Gaijin* sprawled on the sand and a fat man munching a donut and a fat dog nearby staring into the cold, dark distance.

Principle 16: Master Mathematics

Unlike English, mathematics is not a linguistic subject. It has its own language, the language of numbers and formulae which is technical and structured. Success in mathematics is less about brilliant creative expression and lucid arguments. Compared to linguistic subjects, where there are abstract factors at play such as mood, tone and style, mathematics is a far more structured subject. And remember the approach for studying mathematics will also work for other technical and structured subjects such as physics, chemistry and computer science.

Yet, how can I, someone who deals in the written word help you with mathematics? The answer is from my own diverse learning and teaching background. In my university days I completed a degree in accountancy and another degree in English literature simultaneously. During my accountancy degree, I also studied economics and marketing. These subjects required prerequisite study of calculus and statistics.

English and accounting was sometimes a strange combination. There were often moments when an American Poetry anthology would find itself on top of a desk full of ledger accounts. And the students in each department were so different. University English students are an expressive and interesting bunch with diverse styles of dress and conversation. In English tutorials it is not unusual to enjoy tea and cake or spend a pleasant hour debating the realism of a novel. On the other hand accounting tends to be made up of driven professional people who aspire to work in accountancy firms.

However the unique experience of studying a linguistic course and at the same time a mathematical course allowed me to quickly understand the different study methods that were required to succeed in each. At the same time I was also tutoring students in both sides, in English and speech on the linguistic side, and then in accounting, economics and statistics on the mathematical side.

Even though English literature is my favorite subject, I also enjoy mathematics. Mathematics is a beautiful subject in many ways. Unlike English which requires an exhausting and constant stream of creative invention to come up with all the words needed to express oneself accurately, mathematics involves the simple beauty of solving problems through organized systems and innovative approaches.

As you become good in English by learning to express yourself clearly, you become good in Mathematics by learning to solve and find approaches to problems. That's why in principle 5 a Cost Volume Profit mathematical analysis was included where you were asked to calculate the best selling price to make the most profit.

In the subject of English you must exercise the curiosity, imagination and close reading ability to express ideas and answers. In the subject of mathematics you must exercise your minds' logic and problem solving capabilities to understand numbers and create solutions using numbers.

Many students forget that mathematics is also a language, and it is one of the most succinct and powerful languages for communicating numerical information. Today we use averages, means, medians, standard deviations and regression analysis to understand trends in our world. Mathematics is important in business and in science. It is the language of measurement and the language of precision.

What can be seen often is students who are very good at either English or Mathematics but not both subjects. One reason for this is that the top English students try to take a linguistic approach to mathematics, and the top mathematics students try to take a mathematical approach to English.

Mathematics is not a subject where you succeed by relying on your learning and memorization of the concepts and formulae. It is a practical subject like building furniture from wood or playing golf. It is a subject where skill arrives during a journey of constant practice. The lesson here is that the best way to study mathematics is by constant practice. Practice of one aspect of mathematics, leads to skill in other areas.

Mathematics is also a subject where many students are left behind. It is a cumulative subject. Sometimes students miss one crucial concept or methodology in mathematics. Then they lose the ability to complete future problems that rely on that methodology. By way of an important warning in consideration of the nature of the subject, *do not fall behind in mathematics*. So often a spiral develops. Students miss a concept. They fall deeper into a hole of confusion. They begin to think that they're just no good at mathematics. That it's just not their subject. Yet with constant practice and the real desire to stay ahead of what is being taught, mathematics is an easy subject that every student can excel in. Furthermore, mathematics is an objective subject. Unlike English which depends to some degree on subjective opinions, mathematics has answers that are 100% right or 100% wrong. For skilled operators, it is often possible to get 100% in mathematics exams and tests for this very reason.

Angela (not her real name) was a student who struggled in mathematics. It had always been her bottom subject. Wanting to enter a design programme at a polytechnic, she needed a reasonable result in mathematics to guarantee her admittance to the course. With tuition from a dedicated teacher and a good friend of mine, Angela developed confidence in mathematics through practice and a change in mental attitude. The instruction and practice showed her that mathematics could be fun when you developed the skills to solve difficult problems, problems that had previously been obstacles! Angela built confidence and gained some enjoyment in mathematics by gaining good feelings from learning how to solve the problems that had previously stumbled her.

The other secret to success for top students in mathematics is that they gain enjoyment from solving complex puzzles and testing the logical abilities of their mind. Students who perform poorly in mathematics often get frustrated and give up too easily. That's probably because they never reach a state of flow or enjoyment with cracking puzzles. Remember, most problems in mathematics relate to some aspect of life that needs to be calculated out there in the real world, particularly in the areas of business or science. Thus, principle 5, relating it to life is important in mathematics as is principle 2, solve problems and answer questions and principle 12, access a river of flow.

As the top students will tell you, success in mathematics comes with practice, problem solving, interest and more practice.

Principle 17: Master exams, essays & assignments

Throughout the journey and along the way your success as a student is inevitably measured through exams, tests, essays and assignments. The top students know how to approach these assessments. They do not become nervous or stressed by them. They treat them as mere small hurdles to jump, and so often they leap them with grace and flair.

Let's begin with exams and tests. During my school and university life I often found myself dreading test time. I would become nervous. I would find the exams mentally and emotionally exhausting. I can well remember studying on the top floor of the university library, and despite the beautiful sea view, feeling that I wanted to run outside and scream. The long periods of study and revision frustrated me. The exam filled me with anxiety and dread. I wanted the exam to be over, and I wanted the subject to be finished. Yet as the years went by, I found better approaches.

I met other students who walked into exams relaxed and confident. These students even seemed to reach a state of flow during their examinations. They had a different mental picture. They saw the exams as energizing challenges, the way a seasoned rock climber would mountain slopes in summer. And in a way their logic was wise. Exams and tests represent real opportunities to show off your skill to another person. They represent the chance to have your work read and your approaches assessed by another person, skilled in their field. It is in the preparing and going through exams and tests that the edge of your sword becomes sharpened. You have to see the big picture. No matter what grade you get, you are learning and putting in practice your knowledge.

From my own study experience and from my observations of students of all different levels of ability and achievement, here are some important rules in approaching tests and exams:

1. Don't worry, relax

It's as simple as that. Some students spend so much mental energy worrying and stressing over their potential performance, that crowds out the room in their mind to enjoy the concepts they're learning and to reach an accelerated stage of learning and an advanced level of performance. And remember, relax, exams are a lot like dates, when you're relaxed, confident and positive they go a whole lot better, even if you are bluffing at least some of the time.

2. Budget your time

So many students do poorly in exams because they run out of time. It seems such a simple concept, yet the main reason for losing marks is students don't do the questions. And the main reasons they don't do the questions is because they've wasted too much time on other areas that just weren't worth it in terms of marks. Remember, you can't get your ticket clipped if you don't go to the station.

To budget your time for each question work out its percentage of the total mark. For instance if the exam is out of 100%, and question 1 is worth 15 marks, it is thus 15% of the exam. If you have 3 hours or 180 minutes to complete the examination you should only be spending a maximum of 27 minutes on that question, because that's all it is worth. Don't spend 40 minutes on it just because it's tough or you want to show how much extra you know. Move on, move purposefully and budget your time.

3. Find study buddies

I'm not implying that study is some kind of social club, or your school is your friendly neighborhood café, because it is also a place of independent learning and competition. But when you study with friends, compare your results with friends and share the experiences of preparing for and going through major challenges like big tests and exams, the whole experience becomes more fun.

4. Get a coach

Top golfers like Tiger Woods succeed on the golf course because they have a coach. Why would arguably one of the world's best golfers need a coach you might ask? Surely Tiger would know everything there is about the game of golf? Perhaps the reasons are best summed up by Louise Sauvage, the multi medal winning para-olympic champion:

Coaching myself was difficult. I found it hard to monitor my training to make sure I wasn't doing too much or too little. It was hard to be objective.
- Louise Sauvage

The best coach for the student is a tutor who knows the landscape of the subject and how to navigate it. Not only will a good tutor motivate the student and stretch their mind, he or she will also ensure they can do each part well. A dedicated tutor also helps to give students the "Hawthorne Effect" – the feeling that because they are being monitored and coached they have to do better. Top students take additional tutoring and coaching beyond the school classroom through either after school programmes or one-to-one tuition.

Coach Lombardi showed me that by working hard and using my mind, I could overcome my weakness to the point where I could be one of the best.
- The American footballer, Bart Starr on coach Vince Lombardi

Students need tuition and coaching that is dedicated to helping them be the best, whatever level they begin from. Any tuition programme should set realistic goals and then monitor and report on progress, just like in the business world.
- Accelerated Learning Institute (www.acceleratedlearn.com)

5. Enjoy the preparation

Preparing for an exam is when you, the student, come face to face with the full sum of the beauty of the knowledge in your subject. It's a time when you should enjoy real learning. It's the time when under pressure, you will learn the most.

When studying for linguistic exams that require memorization of phrases, dates or concepts, the following formula can work well:

First, build a pile of all the books and notes that could possibly be tested. Begin building your first set of master summary notes. These notes will consist of pages of the important points you must remember. Check dictionaries, other books or the internet on occasion to research further some of the finer or interesting points you discover to truly increase your mastery.

Second, when your master summary note set is complete, perhaps 20-40 pages of notes, then attempt to summarize the main points from these notes into 10-20 pages of refined summary.

Finally, take those 10-20 pages and turn them into 10-20 small cards of memory jogging notes that can be carried with you anywhere, such as on the bus or in the lavatory.

Remember, in mathematical subjects practice, practice and more practice will probably be more important than understanding notes.

To increase your motivation for preparation, a good method is to develop a weekly study timetable and a study log. The timetable will help you focus and the study log will help build your confidence as you see your study hours building. I once had a high school teacher who would collect in our study timetables around exam time. He'd phone up our parents to check we were doing our timetabled studies. Sometimes it was embarrassing when he phoned your mother and asked her what you were doing.

"He's watching TV, or using the computer", was a typical reply.

"Well, well, well" the old teacher would say, "he's supposed to be studying mathematics at this time."

In your study log, reward yourself for achieving blocks of study hours. For instance one student I came across was a basketball freak. He added 1 matchstick to a pile in a tray on his desk for every hour that he studied toward his final exams. 10 matchsticks earned him the reward of some time to go out and shoot hoops. I've seen other students reward themselves with shopping money, $1 per hour studied. But overall, these tricks are really just a bit of fun to entice your mind more. It is most vital that you enjoy your studies, get on a high and achieve principle 12, a state of flow in your test preparation.

The mental approach for essays and assignments is much the same as for tests. However the actual approach can differ. Most essays and assignments require some form of research, reading or close analysis. It is best to do this first and build up your research or analysis notes before you begin. That way you can specialize. When it comes to writing up the assignment or the essay, you will then have everything in front of you and can get to work with focus. Remember principle 7 of achieving complete focus for best results. Structure is very important in essays. Good essays should have an introduction, a body that builds through a sequence of logical points to a deeper level of argument and finally a conclusion that sums up the findings, argument and final answer.

Importantly you must answer the question or fulfill the objectives of the essay or assignment. Top students impress their markers and convince them into awarding their paper an A by showing off what great lengths they go to in order to answer a question. Remember S.E.E., showing, explaining and *proving* with examples. A court of law would not believe you without concrete *proof* and *evidence* so don't expect a tutor or teacher marking your work to either.

Yet as with all these techniques, success and confidence come with focus, flow and practice. If you aim to operate at the top level of study success you will reach it. And when you do reach it, then it will be easy for you to keep operating at that level. Remember learning is lifelong, it is rewarding as knowledge of anything is knowledge of yourself. The biggest thing of all is don't give up. Keep trying. Life is a struggle to reach your potential excellence. But as you journey upward toward your ultimate operating level you will enjoy a real sense of the world being a good and great place.

End of the journey

Thanks for journeying with me. Taking time to learn and to teach has been the most rewarding experience of my life, and I'm still just at the early stages. I want you to succeed in your study and reach your best level of study success, not because I want to load you up with pressure, turn you into a nerd or ensure you become highly paid, but because I want you to have fun.

Remember at the start how I told you this programme is a lot like a pizza: tasty, delivered to your door and in bite size slices – 17 of them actually.

What I didn't tell you is that you have to make, top and cook that pizza. Keep your completed exercises and look back over them as time goes by. Read parts of this book again any time you need a little coaching and encouragement. Be hungry to learn, to stretch your mind, to practice and to get into what you're studying. But most of all don't forget, the pizza will taste great because you're the one who is making it.

Individuals of note

Throughout this book, a number of quotations have been used from notable individuals. Below is a collection of short bios on some of the most important.

Albert Einstein (1879-1955)

Perhaps one of the world's best known scientists, he is best known for his theories of relativity and his hypothesis concerning the particle nature of light. He did not enjoy his early studies at the Swiss Federal Institute of Technology, and would often wag classes to study physics on his own or play the violin. In 1921 he was awarded the Nobel Prize for Physics and became internationally renowned. He left Germany for the United States when Hitler came to power and took a position at the Institute for Advanced Study at Princeton, New Jersey. In 1939 he collaborated with other physicists to write a letter to President Roosevelt warning of the possibility of an atomic bomb and the likelihood that the German government may be seeking to make one. This helped increase the urgency for the US to build such a bomb first, but Einstein did not himself play any role in this work.

Rene Descartes (1596-1650)

Sometimes known as the "father of modern philosophy", Descartes was a French philosopher, scientist and mathematician. After graduating in law and following the beginnings of a military career, Descartes devoted the rest of his life to the study of problems in mathematics and philosophy. He attempted to apply the rational methods of science and mathematics to philosophy, stating that "In our search for the direct road to truth, we should busy ourselves with no object about which we cannot attain a certitude equal to that of the demonstration of arithmetic and geometry." His investigations began with the famous words *Cogito, ergo sum*, "I think, therefore I am."

Helen Keller (1880-1968)

From a very young age Helen Keller became ill and lost both her vision and hearing. At the age of 7, her parents hired a tutor, Anne Sullivan. Sullivan devised a method of making hand signs that Keller could understand, by having the signs pressed into Keller's palm. Keller went on to Radcliffe College, where with Sullivan spelling out lectures into her palms, she obtained a degree. The first deaf and blind person to graduate college, Keller went on to write "The Story of My Life" and traveled the world as a champion for the blind.

Katherine Mansfield (1888-1923)

Born in New Zealand, Katherine Mansfield is regarded as one of the masters of the short story. Her works are taught worldwide due to the revolutionary nature of her prose which shook off the desire to concentrate on plots and endings, instead creating stories which entered ordinary lives, making them vivid and strong. Her fiction is remarkable for its open-endedness and it's ability to raise uncomfortable questions about belonging and identity. Mansfield's adventurous spirit and desire to experiment were hallmarks of her work, and Virginia Woolf once said that Katherine Mansfield had produced "the only writing I had ever been jealous of."

Abraham Maslow (1908-1970)

Maslow was born in Brooklyn, New York, the first of seven children. His parents were uneducated Jewish immigrants from Russia. Hoping for the best for their children in the "new world", they pushed Abraham for academic success. He became lonely as a boy, finding refuge in books. To please his parents he first studied Law at the City College of New York, but throughout the early 1930s he gained his BA, MA and PhD in psychology from the University of Wisconsin. In 1951 he served as the chair of the Psychology Department at Brandeis for 10 years and it was here where he begun his crusade for a humanistic psychology.

Winston Churchill (1874-1965)

A war time leader and outstanding orator, Churchill attended the Royal Military College at Sandhurst and gained commission in the army in 1895. After escaping from capture in the Boer War, he became a national hero and became a Member of Parliament in 1908. Throughout the 1930s he was a back-bench parliamentarian and his career was not helped by his support for Edward VIII in the 1936 abdication crisis. However, in 1940 he succeeded Chamberlain as Prime Minister and became known as a great leader who took Britain from the edge of defeat to victory in World War II. Churchill was also a respected author who won the Nobel Prize for Literature in 1953.

Mahatma Gandhi (1869-1948)

Gandhi studied law in London and returned to India to practice in 1891. In 1893 he went to South Africa to complete a one year legal contract. At that time South Africa was controlled by the British and when Gandhi tried to claim his rights as a British subject he was abused. Noticing that all Indians suffered similar treatment, Gandhi stayed in South Africa for 21 years working for the rights of Indian people. He developed a method of action call Satyagraha, which was based on the principles of courage, non-violence and truth. He returned to India in 1915 and within 15 years had become the leader of the Indian Nationalist movement. Using the principles of Satyagraha he led the campaign for Indian independence from the British and was arrested many times for his activities. He used fasting to demonstrate his dedication to non-violent protest and considered it honorable to go to jail for a just cause. In 1947 India was granted independence, and today Gandhi is honored by many as the father of the Indian nation.

Aristotle (384-322 BC)

Aristotle was the most influential of all the Greek philosophers. He studied under Plato, but differed from him on many points, especially in the fundamental doctrine termed the Theory of Ideas. Aristotle stated that all philosophy must be founded on the observation of facts. He first developed the philosophical ideas of matter, form, time and space, arguing the necessary existence of God as the ultimate cause of all things. At the age of 50 Aristotle opened a school in Athens called the Lyceum, but fled to Euboea when the Macedonian party charged him with impiety.

Somerset Maugham (1874-1965)

W. Somerset Maugham wrote his first novel, *Liza of Lambeth*, during his final year of medical school. This realistic novel drew on his experiences of treating patients from the Lambeth slums of London. The book received some public acclaim, allowing Maugham to abandon his medical career to become a full time writer. A year later he begun a life-long pattern of writing and traveling, becoming one of the most successful writers of all time. However, Maugham had originally seemed destined to become a lawyer, as his father and grandfather had both been prominent attorneys. Yet a severe stutter made him afraid to speak, and an orphan at the age of 10 he was raised by his uncle, a Clergyman. As a youngster he was shy and withdrawn and more of an observer in life, something that he was later able to turn to his advantage as a writer. During World War II he lived in Hollywood where many of his stories and plays were made into movies. After the war Maugham returned to the Villa Mauresque, a home he had purchased on the French Riviera. There he continued to write and entertain the rich and famous.

Oscar Wilde (1854-1900)

Oscar Wilde was educated at Trinity College, Dublin and later at Oxford, where he is said to have discovered the dangerous but delightful aspiration of being different from others. Moving to London in 1879 he set about establishing himself as a leader of the aesthetics movement, and short of money embarked on a lecture tour in America in 1882. With the later publication of The Picture of Dorian Gray (1891) and a string of successful plays, Oscar Wilde became the "toast of London society", idolized for his brilliant wit. However he later met with tragedy, being charged with "homosexual offences" and ending up bankrupt and in prison. In 1897 he was released from prison and left England for France where in 1900 he died a broken man.

Summary of the principles

Principle 1: Stretch your mind
Principle 2: Solve problems & answer questions
Principle 3: Find driving forces/motivational bases
Principle 4: Do each part well
Principle 5: Relate it to life
Principle 6: Learn from failure
Principle 7: Focus for results
Principle 8: Make a plan for the future
Principle 9: Gain total self confidence in studies
Principle 10: Leap the obstacles
Principle 11: Show off your skill
Principle 12: Access a river of flow
Principle 13: Harness the magic of memory
Principle 14: Know your learning style
Principle 15: Master English, reading & writing
Principle 16: Master Mathematics
Principle 17: Master exams, essays & assignments

Bibliography

Angelo, Simon
Click & Grow Rich: Your Pay Packet On The Internet - Earning A Living And
Making Extra Profits In Cyberspace!
Auckland: SurfBrains Books, 2002

Angelo, Simon
Tokyo Curry: A Rhys Rimes Adventure
Auckland: Carlisle Scripts, 2003

Bartol, Kahtryn M. & Martin, David C.
Management
New York: McGraw-Hill, 1994

Beahm, George
The Stephen King Story
Kansas City: Andrews and McMeel, 1991

Carnegie, Dale.
How to Win Friends and Influence People
London: Vermilion, 1998

Clason, George S.
The Richest Man in Babylon
Chicago: Lushena Books, 2001

Dauten, Dale.
The Max Strategy: how a businessman got stuck at an airport and learnt to
make his career take off
New York: William Morrow & Co, 1996

Dryden, Gordon & Voss, Jeanette
The Learning Revolution
Stratford, UK: Network Educational Press, 2001

Gardener, Howard.
Frames of Mind: The Theory of Multiple intelligences
New York: Basic Books, 1983

Gleitman, Henry.
Psychology
New York: W. W. Norton & Co, 1991

Goleman, Daniel.
Emotional Intelligence: why it can matter more than IQ
London: Bloomsbury, 1996

Grudin, Robert.
The Grace of Great Things: creativity and innovation
New York: Ticknor & Fields, 1990

Kiyosaki, Robert T.
Rich Dad's Rich Kid, Smart Kid: giving your child a financial head start
Paradise Valley, Arizona: Tech Press, 2001

Maguire, Jack
Care and Feeding of the Brain: a guide to your gray matter
New York: Doubleday, 1990

Montessori, Maria
The Absorbent Mind
Oxford: Clio, 1998

Oppenheimer, Jerry.
Seinfeld: the making of an American icon
New York: Harper Collins, 2002

Ostrander, Sheila & Schroeder, Lynn with Ostrander, Nancy
Superlearning
New York: Delacorte Press, 1994

Otto, Luther B.
Helping Your Child Choose a Career
Indianopolis: JIST, 1996

Robbins, Anthony
Awaken the Giant Within: how to take immediate control of your mental,
emotional, physical & financial destiny
New York: Simon & Schuster, 1992

Russell, David W.
The Kumon Method of Education
New York: Intercultural Group, 1993

Shakespeare, William
As You Like It
Oxford: Oxford University Press, 1998

Smith, Paul.
Success in New Zealand Business
Auckland: Hodder Moa Beckett, 1996

Steinbeck, John
Of Mice and Men
London: Random House, 1995

Storr, Anthony.
Music and the Mind
London: Harper Collins, 1992

Tolkein, J. R. R.
The Hobbit
London: Harper Collins, 2000

The Holy Bible

The New Zealand Herald

Simon Angelo is available for training, consulting and speaking engagements by appointment. He can be contacted through:

ACCELERATED LEARNING INSTITUTE
Website: www.acceleratedlearn.com
Email: acceleratedlearn@xtra.co.nz
Telephone: +64 9 625 5590

If you would like to order additional copies of *Study Success* for yourself, a friend or as a gift please contact us as above.

When education matters…

Our coaching and education programmes help to improve:
- Self confidence
- Ability to concentrate
- Self discipline
- Overall self esteem

Our unique learning services for children and adults include:
- Class groups in English, Speech & Drama, Mathematics & Science at all levels
- One-to-one teaching in most academic subjects
- Speech & Drama, Public Speaking & Debating and Interview & Negotiation skills
- Computer Training and Sales Training
- Institutional and Corporate training courses
- Curriculum development and Consulting Services
- Life Coaching and Mentoring

Contact us now for you, your child or your organization…

ACCELERATED LEARNING INSTITUTE
Website: www.acceleratedlearn.com
Email: acceleratedlearn@xtra.co.nz
Telephone: +64 9 625 5590